Let Every Tongue Confess

A Mission Reader

Urbana Advance

Edited by Ken Shingledecker
& James E. Berney

InterVarsity Press
Downers Grove
Illinois 60515

Revised edition © 1981 by Inter-Varsity Christian Fellowship of the United States of America.
© 1979 by Inter-Varsity Christian Fellowship of the United States of America.

Original edition issued under the title You Can Tell the World.

InterVarsity Press is the book-publishing division of Inter-Varsity Christian Fellowship, a student movement active on campus at hundreds of universities, colleges and schools of nursing. For information about local and regional activities, write IVCF, 233 Langdon St., Madison, WI 53703.

ISBN 0-87784-497-6

Printed in the United States of America

Library of Congress Cataloging in Publication Data
Main entry under title:

Let every tongue confess.

A handbook to prepare people for Urbana 81, the 13th Inter-Varsity Student Missions Convention, Dec. 27-30, 1981, University of Illinois at Urbana.
"Original edition issued under the title: You can tell the world."
Bibliography: p.
1. Missions—Addresses, essays, lectures. 2. College students in missionary work—Addresses, essays, lectures. 3. Inter-varsity Student Missions Convention, 13th, University of Illinois at Urbana, 1981—Addresses, essays, lectures. I. Shingledecker, Ken, 1951- II. Berney, James E., 1937- III. Inter-varsity Student Missions Convention, 13th, University of Illinois at Urbana, 1981.
BV2030.L47 1981   266   80-28603
ISBN 0-87784-497-6

18 17 16 15 14 13 12 11 10 9 8 7 6 5 4 3 2 1
95 94 93 92 91 90 89 88 87 86 85 84 83 82 81

Preface

It is great to know that you are interested in God's work in the world. By reading this book and studying it in depth, you will be able to decide more effectively on your place in God's world.

The prime purpose of this book is to prepare you to maximize your experience at the Inter-Varsity Christian Fellowship Student Missions Convention to be held the last five days of 1981 at the University of Illinois, Champaign-Urbana. It is commonly known as Urbana 81.

Because Urbana 81 is focused on the topic of God's worldwide mission, you will want to do some thinking and question asking about it ahead of time. This book, especially part three, will also help you with some very practical matters like what kind of clothes to wear for a Midwest winter and how to find your way around campus.

This book is also written so you can grow in your understanding of missions even though you can't attend Urbana. It is organized in four self-contained parts designed to introduce you to four key ideas about world missions.

☐ What missions is all about
☐ Studies in Luke
☐ The practical side of preparing for Urbana
☐ What you can do now about God's mission

A good way to get the main thrust of each article or study is to write a paragraph in a notebook on each when you're done.

Another help would be to discuss this book as a group. At the end are questions for ten group discussions, including the four Bible studies. If you and a few friends are going to Urbana or are just thinking about missions, get together and work your way through these discussions. You might be surprised at what will happen.

Finally pray by name for all those you know who are preparing for or have had an Urbana experience.

For his sake and the world's,
Ken Shingledecker
Inter-Varsity Missions

Prolog:
Inter-Varsity Christian
Fellowship and Urbana

The Urbana missions convention is sponsored by the Inter-Varsity Christian Fellowships of the United States and Canada. It's primary purpose is to glorify Christ by helping students find God's place for them in world missions and thus to serve the church in strengthening its ministry. But Inter-Varsity is much more than Urbana.

Inter-Varsity Is Students

Inter-Varsity is students declaring God's glory on campuses, students living out their faith in Jesus Christ, students united by and rooted in Scripture, students reaching cross-culturally with the gospel.

Inter-Varsity is not a church, it is not a denomination, and it is not a mission board. *Inter-Varsity is part of the church as students and faculty from many denominations in hundreds of student-run campus fellowships commit themselves to follow Christ as Lord.*

What is this fellowship like? Each local "chapter" of IVCF strives to follow Jesus Christ in different ways. Many get together daily to praise God and to pray. In weekly Bible studies they dig into the Word for themselves. Students and faculty also encourage each other to share Christ with non-Christian friends. One faculty member shared Christ in his classes, and this encouraged students to share their faith. A dozen came to Christ as a result.

Inter-Varsity Is Training

But students and faculty are not alone. As a national movement IVCF provides many resources for campus Christians. Take, for example, one of the most important: Inter-Varsity staff members visit campuses to teach from the Scripture, to train in evangelism, to give an example of what it means to follow Christ daily. At one university, a staff member led a discipleship training program for a core of students; from this students started an evangelistic Bible study and began personal evangelism; as a result, a new believer enrolled in the freshman discipleship course held soon after. The spiritual "cycle of life" continues.

Inter-Varsity students are also involved in training camps and conferences. The annual Fort Lauderdale Beach Evangelism Project at Easter, Bible and Life study weekends, and the summer-long Aspen Project are just a few of many.

Various branches of IVCF offer still other resources. The Student Missions Fellowship (SMF) works to present overseas missions at Christian schools. The Nurses Christian Fellowship (NCF) shares the same goals as IVCF as it seeks to help nursing school students and graduates bring Christ into their nursing care. The TWENTYONEHUNDRED team produces multimedia shows for use on campus.

Committed discipleship is encouraged through literature. Inter-Varsity Press and HIS magazine both aim to help the mind grow under Christ's lordship.

Inter-Varsity Is Worldwide Fellowship

Inter-Varsity in Canada and the United States are only two member movements of the worldwide International Fellowship of Evangelical Students (IFES). The movement in Brazil distributes Portuguese literature through bookstores, schools and newsstands in that country and in Portugal. In Nigeria, Christian students recently confronted classmates and others at the International Black Arts Festival with the lordship of Jesus Christ in contrast to the occult. Schloss Mittersill, a castle in the Austrian Alps, bursts at the seams with the international family gathering for training conferences, Bible seminars, and evangelistic house-parties. These are only a few of the many activities of the over 50 national movements joined together in student outreach.

Inter-Varsity Is People

Inter-Varsity is more than Urbana—people on campus and off, salaried and volunteer, from across North America, many churches; people behind the scenes, typing, keeping records, writing, planning, in national, regional and area offices; men and women entrusted with the corporate and legal responsibilities on the corporations and boards of IVCF-USA and IVCF-Canada; business people and homemakers serving on Local Committees to raise the funds needed to support the campus work—all these and more help make up Inter-Varsity.

A Glossary on Missions

Animism—the primitive belief that animals, natural forces (rain, thunder) and inanimate objects possess personal souls often having supernatural powers.

Call—a strong conviction that God wants a person to serve him in some specific way and/or place. This does not usually come through some exotic experience but through prayerful investigation of the possibilities for mission.

Church Growth—a movement within modern missions concerned with multiplication of converts and congregations.

Church planting—the process of beginning local Christian congregations generally in areas where the gospel has not been previously received.

Contextualization—understanding and communicating biblical truth in such a manner that hearers perceive it to be relevant in their culture.

Crosscultural communication—the way people of one society convey ideas to those of another society who differ in such areas as language, values, thought forms and behavior.

Crosscultural evangelism—communicating the good news of Jesus Christ across cultural barriers. Ralph Winter has coined the terms *E-1 Evangelism* (evangelism to non-Christians who have the same culture), *E-2 Evangelism* (evangelism that is crosscultural but able to build on certain overlapping areas, like French and Spanish cultures) and *E-3 Evangelism* (evangelism from one culture to a totally different one) to further clarify the task of crosscultural evangelism.

Culture—the integrated system of learned patterns of behavior, ideas and products characteristic of a society.

Culture shock—the experience of a person who is entering a society very different from the one to which he or she is accustomed. It is sometimes characterized by confusion, physical illness, insecurity, fear of defensiveness.

Deputation—the activity/ministry of missionaries or missionary appointees through which they establish a relationship with sending churches and individuals for prayer and financial support.

Discipling—building up believers and training them to witness to others.

Evangelism—communicating to others the good news of salvation through Jesus Christ.

Expatriate—a person who lives in a country not his or her own.

Faith mission—a mission agency which is not related to a denomination, receiving its personnel and support from denominational and/or unaffilated groups.

Furlough—a period during which the missionary returns to his sending country to gain new perspective, improve skills and renew contact with supporters.

Hinduism—a worldwide religion predominant in India which is characterized by belief in reincarnation and one supreme deity which exists in many forms and natures.

Holistic—emphasizing the needs of the whole person (spiritual, physical, intellectual, social and emotional).

House churches—small groups of Christians, usually with nonprofessional leaders, who meet together as congregations in an individual's house or apartment.

Indigenous church—a church which reflects the culture in which it is located, administering and supporting its own life and outreach.

Islam—the religious faith of Muslims based on the belief that Allah is the sole diety and Muhammad is his prophet.

Liberation theology—a movement in the modern church which emphasizes the need to free men from oppressive economic and social structures.

Mission agency—an organization which furthers crosscultural evangelism and the establishing of new churches by planning strategy for evangelizing some part or parts of the world and recruiting, training and sending missionaries. A *home mission* agency focuses on non-Christians within the country of the agency.

Missionary—a supported worker who is involved in the expansion of the church in a culture other than his or her own. *Career missionaries* (also called professional missionaries) are individuals choosing long-term missionary service. *Short-term missionaries* are individuals involved in missionary service for two years or less. *Summer missionaries* do not join a mission agency but serve as volunteers for three to six months with the purpose of learning about missions firsthand while giving all the assistance they can.

Missions—the activities of a sending church through which it seeks to communicate the gospel across cultural boundaries with a view to establishing churches that will evangelize.

Moratorium on missions—a proposal debated within the church suggesting that all missionaries return to their sending countries in order to allow each nation to thoroughly indigenize its Christian activities. Decisions would be made later by each country about how many missionaries, if any, should return to it.

Nationalization—to convert (a section of industry, agriculture, commerce or the church) from foreign control and ownership to control and ownership by those in the country itself.

Nationals—a more appropriate term than *natives* for the people of another country. *Native* connotes being uncivilized.

Nonprofessional missionaries—(also called *vocational witnesses*) individuals who support themselves in secular, salaried positions abroad with the primary purposes of evangelizing, discipling and planting churches.

Paternalism—treating people in a fatherly or condescending manner; for example, a mission might continue an authority role which inhibits the maturing of the church it has established.

Pioneer evangelism—taking the gospel to areas which have never heard the gospel.

Saturation evangelism—a strategy which involves mobilizing the whole church to concentrate on making Christ known in a given area.

Short-termers—individuals involved in missionary service for two years or less.

Syncretism—the attempt to combine differing religious or philosophical beliefs.

Theological Education by Extension (TEE)—individualized training in the Bible and church-related skills, provided for church leaders where they live and minister.

Third World—nations, especially in Africa, Latin America and Asia, not aligned with communist or capitalist countries. Also called *developing nations*.

Tribalism—a greater loyalty for one's own tribe than for one's country or religion.

Universalism—the belief that all people in the world will eventually be forgiven and be received by God; sometimes referred to as being "implicit" or "anonymous" Christians.

Unreached/unevangelized people—a homogenous group where less than twenty per cent have received or responded to the gospel.

Western nations (or the West)—those countries which are largely influenced by European or American culture.

Part I

Looking at God's World Mission

Ideas about missions that you will find fascinating and controversial.

A. Leonard Tuggy *reveals the differences between the words* missions *and* evangelism.

John R. W. Stott *summarizes God's promise to Abraham and helps us to see a biblical perspective on missions.*

J. Herbert Kane *gives an overview of how the church is growing in the world.*

Ralph D. Winter *helps you understand the task before us.*

Isabelo Magalit *urges Americans to seek three essential qualifications before becoming missionaries.*

Gordon MacDonald *celebrates the church as the beginning and end of our mission. Good reading. This section will really make you think.*

1

Missions and Evangelism: Is There a Difference?

A. Leonard Tuggy

Recently a Christian leader in the Philippines proposed that future evangelistic efforts concentrate on building up small congregations instead of starting new churches. After all, he calculated that if a church building in the Philippines cost $30,000 to build, 200 churches would cost at least $6,000,000 for construction alone—an impossible amount for a small denomination to raise.

He was right in his concern for strengthening existing churches. I believe that local church evangelism to help small congregations become big ones is good New Testament evangelism, but not good New Testament missions.

Missions and evangelism—are they the same? Often these words are used interchangeably. Yet a careful study of the words *evangelism* and *missions* reveals different meanings.

Evangelism—Newsing the Good News

The word *evangelism* originates directly from the New Testament. The New Testament writers frequently used the term *euanggelion*, meaning "good news," as well as the related word *euanggelizomai*, "to evangelize" or spread the good news. Therefore evangelism simply refers to spreading the good news.

What good news needs to be spread everywhere? Philip told the Ethiopian "the good news of Jesus" (Acts 8:35). The news centers around Jesus—his life and teachings, his substitutionary death and his victorious resurrection. This message is news because it recites what God has done through his Son who entered human history. It is good news because it tells what Jesus did to save us from a hopeless human situation.

This good news must be communicated. People can only believe good news they have first heard, and Paul joined the other witnesses of the resurrection in spreading the message. He said, "Whether then it was I or they, so we preach and so you believed."

But the good news did not come in word only. The power and conviction of the Holy Spirit accompanied the words. The message was backed up by the lives of those who preached it. "You know what kind of men we proved to be among you for your sake" (1 Thess. 1:5). Transformed lives firmly established the credibility of the gospel in a world filled with lying religions.

Today, evangelism essentially remains the same activity of spreading the good news, though it is done in a different world. Materially and technologically, the world has changed drastically, but basic human nature has not. Just as in the first century, we find ourselves alienated from God, from others and from ourselves. We need to know that God reconciled the world to himself through Christ. This good news still needs to be communicated.

Once a man described to me his activities in organizing labor unions among factory workers in the Philippines. He felt unions were needed to insure that the workers would be treated justly and paid fairly. He called his work industrial evangelism. But this was *not* evangelism. It was social action.

Once, a Korean pastor took a job as a factory worker in Korea so he could witness to his fellow workers and organize Bible classes among them. These people worked seven days a week and could not go to church; so the church, through this pastor, came to them. Many people came to know Christ through this man's efforts. This is true, biblical, industrial evangelism.

Although a changed world does not demand a changed message, it may require changes in the way it is communicated. Sometimes evangelism is confused with the many methods which are used to accomplish it. Whether evangelism is called witnessing or sharing, personal or mass, in-depth or saturation, the important question remains, Is the good news being effectively communicated?

Geographical, cultural and linguistic barriers affect the methods, but not the essence of evangelism. If the gospel is meaningfully communicated, whether to our next-door neighbor or to an illiterate tribesman in an Indian village, evangelism takes place. People who respond to the good news may join an existing fellowship of believers or be formed into a new church. In either case, evangelism occurred, though church planting might not have.

In Great Commission terminology, evangelism is preaching the gospel. The "go into all the world" dimension of the Commission leads to another term—missions.

Missions—The Sending and the Going

Unlike the word *evangelism,* the word *missions* cannot be traced to the New Testament. The way Christians have used this word through the years must determine its meaning. To make the matter a little more complicated, the singular form *mission* is often used. Do the two forms have different meanings?

Though the word *missions* is more familiar, the word *mission* has a more fundamental meaning. While not a New Testament word, *mission* nevertheless is closely related to the important New Testament concept of sending or being sent. "As the Father has sent me, even so I send you," Jesus said in John 20:21. Jesus was sent into the world to perform a definite mission. And so are we.

17

To explain his mission, Jesus used the words of Isaiah: "The Spirit of the Lord is upon me, because he has anointed me to preach good news to the poor. He has sent me to proclaim release to the captives and recovering of sight to the blind, to set at liberty those who are oppressed, to proclaim the acceptable year of the Lord" (Lk. 4:18-19).

Another summary of Christ's mission is in Matthew 9:35: "And Jesus went about all the cities and villages, teaching in their synagogues and preaching the gospel of the kingdom, and healing every disease and every infirmity."

Just as Christ preached, taught and healed, so should Christians minister to the whole person. Our mission begins with evangelism, but it does not end there. We are to proclaim the good news. We should also teach and minister to people's physical needs. Our mission encompasses all that Christ has sent us into the world to do; but particularly it is to make disciples and build his church.

Though the word *mission* is related to the work of the church, missions (with the *s*) is rich in its associations. Missions includes all the things missionaries do—evangelizing, discipling, teaching, healing, administering, writing and preaching. In missions all of these activities are done in conscious obedience to the Great Commission. This has been the meaning of missions for at least two hundred years.

Because missions grows out of the Great Commission, it focuses on the task of discipling the nations. Therefore the church lies at the heart of missions. Church Growth is the goal of missions. Missions does not consist of many good but aimless activities. Faithful churches reach out in missions to plant new churches or strengthen weak ones. In missions the church faces the world in order to reproduce itself in the world. It responds to the "go into all the world" part of Christ's Commission.

"Going across the ocean does not make a missionary." True, but geography is an important factor in missions. We cannot go unless we physically move. We are sent into a world made up of places. But clearly geography is not the key factor. Taking the gospel across cultural and linguistic barriers is the critical task of modern missions. Geographical distance is incidental to cultural

18

distance. Some people who live across town may be more distant from us culturally and linguistically than some who share a common language and culture on the other side of the world.

For the past two hundred years, mission societies have maintained the work of missions. But even before the rise of modern missions, the church extended itself through small groups of committed Christians. Dedicated communities such as the Moravians were the immediate precursors of the mission societies. In the Middle Ages the church extended itself through the Roman Catholic orders. Missionary monks ministered before the Middle Ages. This pattern can even be traced to the apostolic bands in New Testament times.

A missionary commissioning service in the local church represents missions in action. A crosscultural ministry begins as the church sends out one of its own members to a new assignment. As the missionary moves out in service, the gospel spreads into new areas, new churches spring up and the sending and the going result in the growth of the church as Christ intended.

Is the popular statement, "Every Christian is a missionary" a valid one? If we mean that every believer is sent into the world to be a witness, then, yes, this is a true statement. But in relationship to the work of missions, we are not all missionaries. Believers should all be involved in missions, but only those who are missionaries in the precise meaning of the word are missionaries.

Through the success of missions the church is now firmly planted in almost every country around the world. Missions is now "from six continents to six continents." This is a tremendous tribute to the success of the missionary enterprise, which has now become a worldwide phenomenon.

Recently, Indian church leaders met in Devlali, India for the All India Congress on Mission and Evangelization. In the "Devlali Letter," they take missions as their primary responsibility: "Crosscultural evangelization: We recognize that most evangelistic effort must be directed, not to the two percent who are Christians, but to the vast majority in India. This can only be done by crossing cultural boundaries."

Missions has revolved full circle. Churches planted by missions are now taking the responsibility for their own missions.

Missions and Evangelism—Related but Different

Are missions and evangelism closely related? Definitely. The Great Commission is missions' mandate, and evangelism is at the heart of the Great Commission. To preach the gospel is the reason for the going, and evangelism is the first and critical step in disciple making.

Are missions and evangelism the same? No, in the sense that the part is not the whole. Missions puts feet to evangelism. Missions also brings the complementary ministries needed to complete the work begun by evangelism. Missions reflects the motivation of the apostle Paul who was under obligation to preach the gospel (evangelism), but he "strived to preach the gospel, *not where* Christ was named" (missions).

Evangelism can be done within our own families, our close friends and near neighbors. Missions cannot. Evangelism can help small churches grow larger, but missions should result in new churches in new places.

Without evangelism, missions becomes a hollow effort in religious imperialism. Without missions, evangelism is simply a parochial activity. The gospel is the message, the world is the goal, and the Christian is the instrument.

Both evangelism and missions share a grand end. The "Devlali Letter" expresses this beautifully in its "Biblical Imperative."

"The sure hope and end of all mission and evangelization is the personal return of our Lord to bring in the fullness of His kingdom. It is a false hope that man can bring about utopia on earth by his efforts. God has put all things under the feet of Christ, and we look forward to 'the fullness of time' when he shall 'Unite all things in him, things in heaven and things on earth.' Jesus Christ alone is Saviour, Lord and King."

A. Leonard Tuggy is the Conservative Baptist Foreign Missions Society's overseas secretary for Asia. This article originally appeared in the September 1977 issue of Impact *magazine and is used by permission.*

2

The Living God Is a Missionary God

John R. W. Stott

Millions of people in today's world are extremely hostile to the Christian missionary enterprise. They regard it as politically disruptive (because it loosens the cement which binds the national culture) and religiously narrow-minded (because it makes exclusive claims for Jesus), while those who are involved in it are thought to suffer from a kind of arrogant imperialism. And the attempt to convert people to Christ is rejected as an unpardonable interference in their private lives. "My religion is my own affair," they say. "Mind your own business, and leave me alone to mind mine."

It is essential, therefore, for Christians to understand the grounds on which the Christian mission rests. Only then shall we be able to persevere in the missionary task, with courage and humility, in spite of the world's misunderstanding and opposition.

More precisely, biblical Christians need biblical incentives. For we believe the Bible to be the revelation of God and of his will. So we ask: Has he revealed in Scripture that "mission" is his will for his people? Only then shall we be satisfied. For then it becomes a matter of obeying God, whatever others may think or say. Here we shall focus on the Old Testament, though the entire Bible is rich in evidence for the missionary purpose of God.

The Call of Abraham

Our story begins about four thousand years ago with a man called Abraham, or more accurately, Abram as he was called at that time. Here is the account of God's call to Abraham.

> Now the LORD said to Abram, "Go from your country and your kindred and your father's house to the land that I will show you. And I will make of you a great nation, and I will bless you, and make your name great, so that you will be a blessing. I will bless those who bless you, and him who curses you I will curse; and by you all the families of the earth shall bless themselves." So Abram went, as the LORD had told him; and Lot went with him. Abram was seventy-five years old when he departed from Haran. (Gen. 12:1-4)

God made a promise (a composite promise, as we shall see) to Abraham. And an understanding of that promise is indispensable to an understanding of the Bible and of the Christian mission. These are perhaps the most unifying verses in the Bible; the whole of God's purpose is encapsulated here.

By way of introduction we shall need to consider the setting of God's promise, the context in which it came to be given. Then we shall divide the rest of our study into two. First, *the promise* (exactly what it was that God said he would do) and second—at greater length—*its fulfillment* (how God has kept and will keep his promise). We start, however, with the setting.

Genesis 12 begins: "Now the LORD said to Abram." It sounds abrupt for an opening of a new chapter. We are prompted to ask: "Who is this 'LORD' who spoke to Abram?" and "Who is this 'Abram' to whom he spoke?" They are not introduced into the text out of the blue. A great deal lies behind these words. They are a key which opens up the whole of Scripture. The previous eleven chapters lead up to them; the rest of the Bible follows and fulfills them.

What, then, is the background to this text? It is this. "The LORD" who chose and called Abram is the same Lord who in the beginning created the heavens and the earth, and who climaxed his creative work by making man and woman unique creatures in his own likeness. In other words, we should never allow ourselves to forget that the Bible begins with the universe, not with the planet earth; then with the earth, not with Palestine; then with Adam the father of the human race, not with Abraham the father of the chosen race. Since, then, God is the Creator of the universe, the earth and all mankind, we must never demote him to the status of a tribal deity or petty godling like Chemosh the god of the Moabites, or Milcom (or Molech) the god of the Ammonites, or Baal the male deity, or Ashtoreth the female deity, of the Canaanites. Nor must we suppose that God chose Abraham and his descendants because he had lost interest in other peoples or given them up. Election is not a synonym for élitism. On the contrary, as we shall soon see, God chose one man and his family in order, through them, to bless *all* the families of the earth.

We are bound, therefore, to be deeply offended when Christianity is relegated to one chapter in a book on the world's religions as if it were one option among many, or when people speak of "the Christian God" as if there were others! No, there is only one living and true God, who has revealed himself fully and finally in his only Son Jesus Christ. Monotheism lies at the basis of mission. As Paul wrote to Timothy, "There is one God, and there is one mediator between God and men, the man Christ Jesus" (1 Tim. 2:5).

The Genesis record moves on from the creation of all things by the one God and of human beings in his likeness, to our rebellion against our own Creator and to God's judgment upon his rebel creatures—a judgment which is relieved, however, by his first gospel promise that one day the woman's seed would "bruise," indeed crush, the serpent's head (3:15).

The following eight chapters (Gen. 4—11) describe the dev-

23

astating results of the Fall in terms of the progressive alienation of human beings from God and from our fellow human beings. This was the setting in which God's call and promise came to Abraham. All around was moral deterioration, darkness and dispersal. Society was steadily disintegrating. Yet God the Creator did not abandon the human beings he had made in his own likeness (Gen. 9:6). Out of the prevailing godlessness he called one man and his family, and promised to bless not only them but through them the whole world. The scattering would not proceed unchecked; a grand process of ingathering would now begin.

The Promise

What then was the promise which God made to Abraham? It was a composite promise consisting of several parts.

First, it was the promise of *a posterity*. He was to go from his kindred and his father's house, and in exchange for the loss of his family God would make of him "a great nation." Later in order to indicate this, God changed his name from "Abram" ("exalted father") to "Abraham" ("father of a multitude") because, he said to him, "I have made you the father of a multitude of nations" (17:5).

Second, it was the promise of *a land*. God's call seems to have come to him in two stages, first in Ur of the Chaldees while his father was still alive (11:31; 15:7) and then in Haran after his father had died (11:32; 12:1). At all events he was to leave his own land, and in return God would show him another country.

Third, it was the promise of *a blessing*. Five times the words *bless* and *blessing* occur in 12:2-3. The blessing God promised Abraham would spill over upon all mankind.

A posterity, a land and a blessing. Each of these promises is elaborated in the chapters that follow Abraham's call.

First, *the land*. After Abraham had generously allowed his nephew Lot to choose where he wanted to settle (he selected the fertile Jordan valley), God said to Abraham: "Lift up your eyes, and look from the place where you are, northward and southward and eastward and westward; for all the land which you see I will give to you and to your descendants for ever" (13:14-15).

Second, *the posterity.* A bit later God gave Abraham another visual aid, telling him to look now not to the earth but to the sky. On a clear, dark night he took him outside his tent and said to him, "Look toward heaven and number the stars." What a ludicrous command! Perhaps Abraham started, "1, 2, 3, 5, 10, 20, 30 . . . ," but he must soon have given up. It was an impossible task. Then God said to him: "So shall your descendants be." And we read: "He believed the Lord." Although he was probably by now in his eighties, and although he and Sarah were still childless, he yet believed God's promise and God "reckoned it to him as righteousness." That is, because he trusted God, God accepted him as righteous in his sight.

Third, *the blessing.* "I will bless you." Already God has accepted Abraham as righteous or (to borrow the New Testament expression) has "justified him by faith." No greater blessing is conceivable. It is the foundation blessing of the covenant of grace, which a few years later God went on to elaborate to Abraham: "I will establish my covenant between me and you and your descendants after you . . . for an everlasting covenant, to be God to you and to your descendants after you . . . and I will be their God" (17:7-8). And he gave them circumcision as the outward and visible sign of his gracious covenant or pledge to be their God. It is the first time in Scripture that we hear the covenant formula which is repeated many times later: "I will be their God and they shall be my people."

A land, a posterity, a blessing. "But what has all that to do with mission?" you may be asking with impatience. My answer is "Everything! Be patient a little longer and you will see." Let us turn now from the promise to the fulfillment.

The Fulfillment

The whole question of the fulfillment of Old Testament prophecy is a difficult one in which there is often misunderstanding and not a little disagreement. Of particular importance is the principle, with which I think all of us will agree, that the New Testament writers themselves understood Old Testament prophecy to have not a *single* but usually a *triple* fulfillment—past, present and future. The

25

past fulfillment was an immediate or historical fulfillment in the life of the nation of Israel. The present is an intermediate or gospel fulfillment in Christ and his church. The future will be an ultimate or eschatological fulfillment in the new heaven and the new earth.

God's promise to Abraham received an immediate, historical fulfillment in his physical descendants, the people of Israel.

God's promise to Abraham of a numerous, indeed of an innumerable, posterity was confirmed to his son Isaac (26:4, "as the stars of heaven") and his grandson Jacob (32:12, "as the sand of the sea"). Gradually the promise began to come literally true. Perhaps we could pick out some of the stages in this development.

The first concerns the years of slavery in Egypt, of which it is written, "The descendants of Israel were fruitful and increased greatly; they multiplied and grew exceedingly strong; so that the land was filled with them" (Ex. 1:7; cf. Acts 7:17). The next stage I will mention came several hundred years later when King Solomon called Israel "a great people, that cannot be numbered or counted for multitude" (1 Kings 3:8). A third stage was some three hundred fifty years after Solomon; Jeremiah warned Israel of impending judgment and captivity, and then added this divine promise of restoration: "As the host of heaven cannot be numbered and the sands of the sea cannot be measured, so I will multiply the descendants of David my servant" (33:22).

So much for Abraham's posterity; what about the land? Again we note with worship and gratitude God's faithfulness to his promise. For it was in remembrance of his promise to Abraham, Isaac and Jacob that he first rescued his people from their Egyptian slavery and gave them the territory which came on that account to be called "the promised land" (Ex. 2:24; 3:6; 32:13), and then restored them to it some seven hundred years later after their captivity in Babylon. Nevertheless, neither Abraham nor his physical descendants fully inherited the land. As Hebrews 11 puts it, they "died in faith, *not* having received what was promised." Instead, as "strangers and exiles on the earth" they "looked forward to the city which has foundations, whose builder and maker is God" (see Heb. 11:8-16, 39-40).

God kept his promises about the posterity and the land, at least in part. Now what about the blessing? Well, at Sinai God confirmed and clarified his covenant with Abraham, and pledged himself to be Israel's God (for example, Ex. 19:3-6). And throughout the rest of the Old Testament God went on blessing the obedient while the disobedient fell under his judgment.

Perhaps the most dramatic example comes at the beginning of Hosea's prophecy, in which Hosea is told to give his three children names which describe God's awful and progressive judgment on Israel. His firstborn (a boy) he called "Jezreel," meaning "God will scatter." Next came a daughter "Lo-ruhamah," meaning "not pitied," for God said he would no longer pity or forgive his people. Lastly he had another son "Lo-ammi," meaning "not my people," for God said they were not now his people. What terrible names for the chosen people of God! They sound like a devastating contradiction of God's eternal promise to Abraham.

But God does not stop there. For beyond the coming judgment there would be a restoration, which is described in words which once more echo the promise to Abraham: "Yet the number of the people of Israel shall be like the sand of the sea, which can be neither measured nor numbered" (Hos. 1:10). And then the judgments implicit in the names of Hosea's children would be reversed. There would be a gathering instead of a scattering ("Jezreel" is ambiguous and can imply either), "not pitied" would be pitied, and "not my people" would become "sons of the living God" (1:10—2:1).

The wonderful thing is that the apostles Paul and Peter both quote these verses from Hosea. They see their fulfillment not just in a further multiplication of Israel but in the inclusion of the Gentiles in the community of Jesus: "Once you were no people but now you are God's people; once you had not received mercy but now you have received mercy" (1 Pet. 2:10; cf. Rom. 9:25-26).

This New Testament perspective is essential as we read the Old Testament prophecies. For what we miss in the Old Testament is any clear explanation of just *how* God's promised blessing would overflow from Abraham and his descendants to "all families of the earth." Although Israel is described as "a light to lighten the nations," and has a mission to "bring forth justice to the nations" (Is. 42:1-4, 6; 49:6), we do not actually see this happening. It is only in the Lord Jesus himself that these prophecies are fulfilled, for only in his day are the nations actually included in the redeemed community. To this we now turn.

God's promise to Abraham receives an intermediate or gospel fulfillment in Christ and his church.

Almost the first word of the whole New Testament is the word *Abraham.* For Matthew's Gospel begins: "The book of the genealogy of Jesus Christ, the son of David, the son of Abraham. Abraham was the father of Isaac. . . ." So it is right back to Abraham that Matthew traces the beginning not just of the genealogy but of the gospel of Jesus Christ. He knows that what he is recording is the fulfillment of God's ancient promises to Abraham some two thousand years previously. (See also Lk. 1:45-55, 67-75.)

Yet from the start Matthew recognizes that it isn't just *physical* descent from Abraham which qualifies people to inherit the promises, but a kind of *spiritual* descent, namely, repentance and faith in the coming Messiah. This was John the Baptist's message to crowds who flocked to hear him: "Do not presume to say to yourselves, 'We have Abraham as our father'; for I tell you, God is able from these stones to raise up children to Abraham" (Mt. 3:9; Lk. 3:8; cf. Jn. 8:33-40). The implications of his words would have shocked his hearers since "it was the current belief that no descendant of Abraham could be lost" (J. Jeremias, *Jesus' Promise to the Nations,* SCM Press, 1958, p. 48).

And God has raised up children to Abraham, if not from stones, then from an equally unlikely source, namely, the Gentiles! So Matthew, although the most Jewish of all four Gospel writers, later records Jesus as having said, "I tell you, many will come from east and west and sit at table with Abraham, Isaac, and Jacob in the kingdom of heaven, while the sons of the kingdom will be thrown into the outer darkness" (8:11-12; cf. Lk. 13:28-29).

It is hard for us to grasp how shocking, how completely topsy-turvy, these words would have sounded to the Jewish hearers of John the Baptist and Jesus. *They* were the descendants of

Abraham; so *they* had a title to the promises which God made to Abraham. Who then were these outsiders who were to share in the promises, even apparently usurp them, while they themselves would be disqualified? They were indignant. They had quite forgotten that part of God's covenant with Abraham promised an overspill of blessing to *all* the nations of the earth. Now the Jews had to learn that it was in relation to Jesus the Messiah, who was himself seed of Abraham, that all the nations would be blessed.

The apostle Peter seems at least to have begun to grasp this in his second sermon, just after Pentecost. In it he addressed a Jewish crowd with the words: "You are the sons . . . of the covenant which God gave to your fathers, saying to Abraham, 'And in your posterity shall all the families of the earth be blessed.' God, having raised up his servant [Jesus], sent him to you first, to bless you in turning every one of you from your wickedness" (Acts 3:25-26). It is a very notable statement because he interprets the blessing in the moral terms of repentance and righteousness and because, if Jesus was sent "first" to the Jews he was presumably sent next to the Gentiles, whose "families of the earth" had been "far off" (cf. Acts 2:39) but were now to share in the blessing.

It was given to the apostle Paul, however, to bring this wonderful theme to its full development. For he was called and appointed to be the apostle to the Gentiles, and to him was revealed God's eternal but hitherto secret purpose to make Jews and the Gentiles "fellow heirs, members of the same body, and partakers of the promise in Christ Jesus through the gospel" (Eph. 3:6).

Negatively, Paul declares with great boldness, "Not all who are descended from Israel belong to Israel, and not all are children of Abraham because they are his descendants" (Rom. 9:6-7).

Who then are the true descendants of Abraham, the true beneficiaries of God's promises to him? Paul does not leave us in any doubt. They are believers in Christ of whatever race. In Romans 4 he points out that Abraham not only received justification by faith but also received this blessing *before he had been circumcised.* Therefore Abraham is the father of all those who, whether circumcised or uncircumcised (that is, Jews or Gentiles), "follow the example of [his] faith" (Rom. 4:9-12). If we "share the faith of Abraham," then "he is the father of us all, as it is written, 'I have made you the father of many nations' " (vv. 16-17). Thus neither physical descent from Abraham, nor physical circumcision as a Jew, makes a person a true child of Abraham, but rather faith. Abraham's real descendants are believers in Jesus Christ, whether racially they happen to be Jews or Gentiles.

What then is the "land" which Abraham's descendants inherit? The letter to the Hebrews refers to a "rest" which God's people enter now by faith (Heb. 3—4). And in a most remarkable expression Paul refers to "the promise to Abraham and his descendants, that they should *inherit the world*" (Rom. 4:13). One can only assume he means the same thing as when to the Corinthians he writes that in Christ "all things are yours, whether Paul or Apollos or Cephas or the world or life or death or the present or the future, all are yours" (1 Cor. 3:21-23). Christians by God's wonderful grace are joint heirs with Christ of the universe.

Somewhat similar teaching, both about the nature of the promised blessing and about its beneficiaries, is given by Paul in Galatians 3. He first repeats how Abraham was justified by faith, and then continues: "So you see that it is men of faith who are the sons of Abraham" and who therefore "are blessed with Abraham who had faith" (vv. 6-9). What then is the blessing with which all the nations were to be blessed (v. 8)? In a word, it is the blessing of salvation. We were under the curse of the law, but Christ has redeemed us from it by becoming a curse in our place, in order "that in Christ Jesus the blessing of Abraham might come upon the Gentiles, that we might receive the promise of the Spirit through faith" (vv. 10-14). Christ bore our curse that we might inherit Abraham's blessing, the blessing of justification (v. 8) and of the indwelling Holy Spirit (v. 14). Paul sums it up in the last verse of the chapter (v. 29): "If you are Christ's, then you are Abraham's offspring, heirs according to promise."

But we have not quite finished yet. There is a third stage of fulfillment still to come. *God's promise to Abraham will receive an ultimate or eschatological fulfillment in the final destiny of all the redeemed.*

30

In the book of Revelation there is one more reference to God's promise to Abraham (7:9ff). John sees in a vision "a great multitude which no man could number." It is an international throng, drawn "from every nation, from all tribes and peoples and tongues." And they are "standing before the throne," the symbol of God's kingly reign. That is, his kingdom has finally come, and they are enjoying all the blessings of his gracious rule. He shelters them with his presence. Their wilderness days of hunger, thirst and scorching heat are over. They have entered the promised land at last, described now not as "a land flowing with milk and honey" but as a land irrigated from "springs of living water" which never dry up. But how did they come to inherit these blessings? Partly because they have "come out of the great tribulation" (evidently a reference to the Christian life with all its trials and sufferings), but mostly because "they have washed their robes and made them white in the blood of the Lamb," that is, they have been cleansed from sin and clothed with righteousness through the merits of the death of Jesus Christ alone. "*Therefore* are they before the throne of God."

Speaking personally, I find it extremely moving to glimpse this final fulfillment in a future eternity of that ancient promise of God to Abraham. All the essential elements of the promise may be detected. For here are the spiritual descendants of Abraham, a "great multitude which no man could number," as countless as the sand on the seashore and as the stars in the night sky. Here too are "all the families of the earth" being blessed, for the numberless multitude is composed of people from every nation. Here also is the promised land, namely, all the rich blessings which flow from God's gracious rule. And here above all is Jesus Christ, the seed of Abraham, who shed his blood for our redemption and who bestows his blessings on all those who call on him to be saved.

Conclusion

Let me try to summarize what we learn about God from his promise to Abraham and its fulfillment.

First, he is the God of history. History is not a random flow of events. For God is working out in time a plan which he conceived

31

in a past eternity and will consummate in a future eternity. In this historical process Jesus Christ as the seed of Abraham is the key figure. Let's rejoice that if we are Christ's disciples we are Abraham's descendants. We belong to his spiritual lineage. If we have received the blessings of justification by faith, acceptance with God, and of the indwelling Spirit, then we are beneficiaries today of a promise made to Abraham four thousand years ago.

Second, he is the God of the covenant. That is, God is gracious enough to make promises, and he always keeps the promise he makes. He is a God of steadfast love and faithfulness. Mind you, he does not always fulfill his promises immediately. Abraham and Sarah "died in faith, *not* having received what was promised, but having seen it and greeted it from afar" (Heb. 11:13). That is, although Isaac was born to them in fulfillment of the promise, their seed was not yet numerous, nor was the land given to them, nor were the nations blessed. All God's promises come true, but they are inherited "through faith *and patience*" (Heb. 6:12). We have to be content to wait for God's time.

Third, he is the God of blessing. "I will bless you," he said to Abraham (Gen. 12:2). "God . . . sent him [Jesus] to you first, to bless you," echoed Peter (Acts 3:26). God's attitude to his people is positive, constructive, enriching. Judgment is his "strange work" (Is. 28:21). His principal and characteristic work is to bless people with salvation.

Fourth, he is the God of mercy. I have always derived much comfort from the statement of Rev. 7:9 that the company of the redeemed in heaven will be "a great multitude which no man could number." I do not profess to know how this can be, since Christians have always seemed to be a rather small minority. But Scripture states it for our comfort. Although no biblical Christian can be a universalist (believing that all mankind will ultimately be saved), since Scripture teaches the awful reality and eternity of hell, yet a biblical Christian can—even must—assert that the redeemed will somehow be an international throng so immense as to be countless. For God's promise is going to be fulfilled, and Abraham's seed is going to be as innumerable as the dust of the earth, the stars of the sky and the sand on the seashore.

Fifth, he is the God of mission. The nations are not gathered in automatically. If God has promised to bless "all the families of the earth," he has promised to do so "through Abraham's seed" (Gen. 12:3; 22:18). Now *we* are Abraham's seed by faith, and the earth's families will be blessed only if *we* go to them with the gospel. That is God's plain purpose.

I pray that these words, "all the families of the earth," may be written on our hearts. It is this expression more than any other which reveals the living God of the Bible to be a missionary God. It is this expression too which condemns all our petty parochialism and narrow nationalism, our racial pride (whether white or black), our condescending paternalism and arrogant imperialism. How dare we adopt a hostile or scornful or even indifferent attitude to any person of another color or culture if our God is the God of "all the families of the earth"? We need to become global Christians with a global vision, for we have a global God.

So may God help us never to forget his four-thousand-year-old promise to Abraham: "By you and your descendants *all* the nations of the earth shall be blessed."

John R. W. Stott has a worldwide ministry as a Bible expositor and writer. The best known of his many books is Basic Christianity. *This article was condensed from a talk given at the Urbana 76 missions convention which appeared in* Declare His Glory *among the Nations. ©1977 by Inter-Varsity Christian Fellowship of the U.S.A.*

3

What in the World Is God Doing?

J. Herbert Kane

In the nineteenth century, thanks to the colonial system, missionaries were able to come and go as they pleased without passports, visas, residence permits and other forms of red tape; but when they entered those wide-open doors they found the hearts of the people closed against them. In the latter half of the twentieth century the shoe is on the other foot. The political doors are sometimes difficult to enter, but once inside, missionaries find the hearts of the people are wide open. One thing is clear. God is doing a new work in our day and we had better get with him if we want a piece of the action.

Never before in history have the non-Christian peoples of the world been so open to the claims of Jesus Christ. Millions of people in all walks of life are showing an unprecedented interest in the Christian faith. Animists in Africa, Hindus in India, Buddhists in Southeast Asia and even Muslims in the Middle East are reading Christian literature, listening to gospel broadcasts and enrolling in Bible correspondence courses in record numbers. Everywhere the Holy Spirit is at work, creating a genuine hunger for the Bread of Life. And this quest for spiritual reality is not confined to the poverty-stricken masses whose interest in religion might be suspect. It includes teachers, students, government officials, successful business and professional people whose hearts have been touched by the Holy Spirit.

The Third-World Church: Vigorous and Vital
With few exceptions the churches in the Third World are throbbing with vigor and vitality. Missionaries on furlough are using two adjectives to describe the exciting situation in many parts of the world—*fabulous* and *fantastic*. Today the cutting edge of the Christian church is in the Third World. That's where the growth is taking place. Some of the "daughter" churches overseas are now larger than the "mother" churches in the West.

It is estimated that in Black Africa some 20,000 persons are embracing Christianity every day. In many churches the Sunday morning congregation is five times larger than the membership. For the first time in history Christians outnumber both the animists and the Muslims. While a significant percentage is evangelical, many are only nominally Christian.

In Korea six new churches come into existence every day. In Seoul one local church has 30,000 members; another has 75,000. In Brazil some 3,000 new congregations are springing up every year. The largest single congregation in the world is in Santiago, Chile—with 80,000 members! In Indonesia the churches are growing so rapidly that pastors and missionaries have been unable to provide adequate training for all those who want to join the church. In some parts of the Third World one ordained pastor has the oversight of a dozen congregations. Under such conditions he can do little more than administer baptism and communion.

Three New Movements
In the 1960s three new movements got under way—Saturation evangelism, Church Growth and Theological Education by Exten-

sion. All three are proceeding under full steam on a worldwide scale with results that ten years ago seemed impossible.

Saturation evangelism, which began in Latin America, has more recently spread to all parts of the world, where it is known by various names. Wherever it has gone it has brought tens of millions within sound of the gospel, resulting in church growth on an enormous scale. One mission leader, after a visit to Africa, wrote: "In some areas where New Life For All campaigns have been held there has been a 50 percent church growth in one year. The results are fantastic but can only be preserved with thorough follow-up by the churches."

The Church Growth movement has gone into orbit in recent years. Church Growth workshops have been held in 45 countries. Resource personnel have been unable to respond to the many calls that have come from all parts of the world. Vergil Gerber's book *God's Way to Keep a Church Going and Growing* has been published in 35 languages, with as many more on the way.

Theological Education by Extension, which began in Guatemala in 1960, aims to provide basic theological training for older pastors who cannot leave home, church, and farm or business to attend Bible school. By 1965 one hundred students had enrolled in the program. Ten years later there were 300 TEE institutions in 75 countries with a total enrollment of 40,000. Only persons who have served on the mission field can possibly appreciate the significance of this development.

Technology and Translation

Modern technology has made it possible to proclaim the good news to all the world. Today there are 65 radio stations owned and operated by Christian missions in the Third World. Most of these are small with local coverage. Others are large and powerful enough to beam the gospel around the world by short wave. One of these stations in Manila is broadcasting the gospel daily from 27 transmitters in 72 languages to more than two billion people in Asia. Every month 18,000 letters are received from almost 60 countries. More than 1,500,000 have enrolled in Bible correspondence courses. The operation requires a full-time staff of 400.

Another exciting venture is the translation of the Scriptures into over 1,660 languages. The complete Bible is now available in languages spoken by 90 per cent of the world's population: the

Some Facts and Figures

World Population. Now stands at 4.3 billion. Annual increase is 1.9%. Christians account for slightly less than 30%. There are more non-Christians in India and China than there are Christians in the entire world.

Christian Population. Estimated at 1.24 billion. Includes 740 million Roman Catholics, 400 million Protestants, and 100 million Eastern Orthodox. Evangelicals may number as many as 200 million.

Protestant Missions. Total number of missionaries—56,500. Divided as follows: From North America 37,000; United Kingdom 7,000; Europe 5,500; Third World 4,000; Other 3,000.

Roman Catholic Missions. Total number of missionaries—65,000. Of these 6,600 are from the U.S.A., down from a peak of 9,655 in 1968. American missionaries are supported by 240 different missions and orders.

American Missions. Mainline denominations (with few exceptions) are retrenching rapidly. Evangelical missions continue to expand. Recruitment is a continuing problem. Older societies, due to deaths and retirements, are barely holding their own. Younger societies are still forging ahead.

World Christianity. Christianity is losing ground in Europe; barely holding its own in North America; doing fairly well in Asia (outside China); gaining ground in Latin America; and registering phenomenal gains in Black Africa.

Muslim World. Apart from Indonesia the Muslim world has yielded few converts to Christianity. Several Muslim countries are closed to Christian missionaries—Saudi Arabia, Syria, Libya, Somalia, Mauritania, South Yemen. Several Arab countries are using their fabulous oil revenues to promote the spread of Islam, especially in Black Africa. Some 25 million Muslims now reside in Europe where they are making their presence felt. The Islamic Revolution in Iran in 1979 may well spark similar movements in other Muslim countries. In spite of this, however, there is reason for cautious optimism regarding the future of evangelical missions to the Muslim world.

Communist World. Some 1.3 billion persons now live under Communism. All suffer some degree of religious persecution. Missionaries, of course, are excluded; but national Christians continue to witness courageously. In the U.S.S.R. there are 40 million Orthodox Christians, 5 million evangelicals, 3 million Roman Catholics, and a million Lutherans. The last two groups are found in Estonia, Latvia, and Lithuania. Contrary to popular opinion, Bibles are published and distributed in small quantities behind the Iron Curtain. In China, Albania, and North Korea the institutional church has been destroyed. With the "Normalization of relations" between China and the U.S.A. in early 1979 there are faint but encouraging signs that the Peking government *may* be getting ready to grant the religious freedom guaranteed by their constitution. It is just possible that a select group of missionaries may be permitted to return to China.

New Testament in another 5 per cent; and at least one book in another 3 per cent. This leaves only 2 per cent without any vernacular portions of the Word of God. The task, however, is far from finished. There are still well over 3,000 tribes still waiting for John 3:16 in their own language. Scores of missions and hundreds of missionaries are now at work on this last frontier.

In the past it was taken for granted that the task of world evangelization was the "white man's burden." In recent years the "younger" churches of the Third World have begun to take responsibility for this work. Today some 4,000 non-Caucasian missionaries are serving in crosscultural situations, most of them supported by their own churches. There is every indication that these churches intend to accept their full share of responsibility for the evangelization of the world. This is one of the most exciting developments of twentieth-century missions.

Jesus said, "The harvest is plentiful, but the laborers are few" (Lk. 10:2). This was never truer than it is today. From every part of the world come calls for help. To meet the desperate need for additional personnel, mission boards have had to depend increasingly on short-term missionaries. The term usually lasts from one to three years. Over six thousand short-termers are now serving overseas. This means that 16 per cent of all Protestant missionaries from North America are now short-termers; 25 per cent of them sign up as career missionaries when their term of service is over.

And so it goes. All around the world the Christian church is on the move—teaching, preaching, helping, healing, building, growing. For the first time in history we have the tools and the techniques to finish the job of world evangelization in one generation. The only problem is *manpower*. Can we get the right kind of missionary in sufficient numbers to complete the task?

In his return from a recent world tour one Christian statesman said: "The more I see of what God is doing in the world, the more I am convinced that we stand today, *at this very hour,* on the threshold of the greatest spiritual advance the world has ever witnessed. Clearly God is telling us that tens of millions are ready and waiting to know Jesus Christ."

J. Herbert Kane is visiting professor of missions and evangelism at Trinity Evangelical Divinity School. This article is © by the Evangelical Missions Information Service (E.M.I.S.) and reprinted with permission of E.M.I.S., Box 794, Wheaton, IL 60187.

4

The Need in
World Mission Today

Ralph D. Winter

As we prepare to confront the future of world mission, before we do anything else, we must sum up our progress to the present. This leads us to an awesome awareness of the task as yet unfinished, that is, the need.

At the International Congress on World Evangelization at Lausanne, I gave an address, the central thesis of which can be summed up in a single sentence: *while there are 2.7 billion people who do not even call themselves Christians, over three-quarters of them are beyond the range of any kind of normal (cultural-near-neighbor) evangelization by existing churches.*

By "normal evangelism" I do not mean what is normally now being done; I refer to all of those various kinds of evangelism which believers in presently existing congregations *would be capable of launching* without surmounting unusual barriers of language and social structure. This has also been called cultural-near-neighbor evangelism or monocultural evangelization or E-0 or E-1 evangelism. E-0 evangelism is winning *nominal Christians* to Christ, and E-1 evangelism is winning people *who do not call themselves Christians* but who are in the same cultural sphere as the church. These surely must continue and must be vastly expanded.

But even assuming a great spiritual evangelizing revival were to sweep every existing congregation in the world, those congregations reaching out in normal evangelism would still be stopped short by cultural barriers before reaching three-fourths of the non-Christians in the world today: *from that point on,* cross-cultural, E-2 (evangelism that is cross-cultural but able to build on certain overlaps, like French and Spanish cultures) and E-3 (evangelism from one culture to a totally different one) would be necessary.

The Three Major Blocs

Figure 1 is a fairly exact scale drawing (as are all the figures in this article, adapted from the table on p. 52) representing the largest racial and cultural bloc of humanity—the Chinese. The large circle on the right represents those Chinese who do not consider themselves Christians. The small circle to the left represents the number of Chinese who do consider themselves Christians. The circle

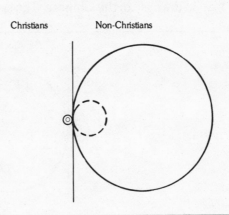

Christians   Non-Christians

Figure 1. The Chinese People

within the left-hand circle represents an estimate of the number of truly committed Chinese Christians by whom I do not mean, for example, all who call themselves evangelicals, but rather truly committed believers, specifically *those Christians on whom we may count to help finish the task.*

The first impression this diagram of the Chinese gives us is the vastness of the unfinished task. But a startling second message comes through when we note that the dotted circle within the large right-hand circle represents the limited number of Chinese whom even cross-cultural evangelists are able to reach during this present epoch of history; that is, the dotted circle represents the 38 million Chinese outside mainland China. But even if China were open, there is in Chinese society an amazing mosaic of subcultural barriers which would put most Chinese beyond the reach of normal evangelism as we have defined it.

Another large bloc of non-Christians is the Hindu. In Figure 2 the large circle again represents non-Christians, this time the number of Hindus who do not consider themselves Christians. Note that here, as in the case of the Chinese, I am referring to a culturally, not a racially or a religiously, defined group. Thus we may say that the left-hand circle represents the number of people of Hindu cultural background who consider themselves Christians. Note carefully that this Christian circle is proportionately larger than in the case of the Chinese. The sphere within the small

Christians   Non-Christians

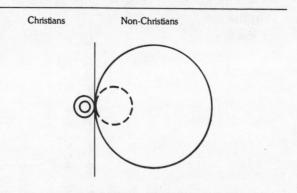

Figure 2. The Hindu People

circle (the committed Christians) is larger too, yet it is smaller relative to the total number of Christians; that is, there are more nominal Christians of Hindu background both absolutely and relatively.

Once more, if we are sensitive at all to the heart of God, we must be stunned and crushed by the vastness of the unreached populations within this major bloc of mankind. But the second message is again more shocking: it is the stubborn fact not often recognized that only a relatively small number of people in India are reachable by normal evangelistic efforts on the part of even the Christians in India. These reachable people, represented by the dotted circle, are the Harijans—the remaining non-Christian peoples in the formerly "untouchable" category.

Let me repeat that by *normal* I do not mean what is now normally being done. A reliable—but staggering—report indicates that 98% of all current evangelistic efforts in India, whether missionary or national, are not even focused on non-Christians, but (as is true in the United States) are attempts of *believing* Christians to reach *nominal* Chirstians and bring them back into the vital fellowship of the church. In terms of the figure, it is Christians of the inner sphere reaching nominal Christians in the doughnut-shaped space around them. These are specifically *not* efforts to reach even the people in the dotted circle, the non-Christians of Hindu culture *who are culturally approachable* by Christians, people with the same cultural traditions—shall we say *caste?*

On the one hand, then, Christians in India are not (with only rare exceptions) even *attempting* to win totally non-Christian people. But on the other hand, if the Christians of India did suddenly and strenuously reach out to every last person within their various cultural traditions, they would not even in that hypothetical case be able to win anyone outside of the dotted circle unless, note, *unless* they made new beachheads by the utilization of what would substantially be traditional missionary techniques (involving the establishment of the kind of professional agencies capable of crossing serious cultural barriers).

All countries have their caste systems. Sometimes the barriers are linguistic differences, economic differences or other types of cultural differences. The barriers of this type are almost always socially describable. They are not spiritual barriers. While the spiritual barriers are the same whether a nominal Christian becomes committed to Christ or a total non-Christian becomes committed to Christ, the cultural barriers, where they exist, are always a stubborn technical problem *in addition.*

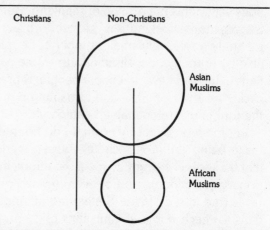

Figure 3. The Muslim People

The third large non-Christian cultural tradition is pictured in Figure 3. Since there are huge numbers of Muslims both in Africa and Asia, we have used two circles to depict the non-Christians of Muslim cultural background. In this case a curious and tragic fact appears: there are not enough Christians of Muslim extraction that we can even depict them in a small circle as we did for the Chinese and the Hindus.

Up to now in mission history we have either not *known* how or have not been *able* to achieve the development of a "Muslims for Jesus" movement anywhere, with one or two possible exceptions. While we have from ten to thirty thousand Christians of Jewish heritage in the United States, despite the fact that they were brought up from infancy to react against the name of Jesus Christ, the amazing fact is that Muslims are brought up to revere Jesus highly. Their holy book, the Koran, technical scholars today point out, actually elevates Jesus above Mohammed. But to date there are very few Muslims for Jesus.

We have now seen three major blocs of non-Christians, and in each case only a tiny proportion of the people in these blocs represent people whose social groupings would allow them easily to become part of (and also attract their friends to) any existing congregation of believers in Christ. To sum up, normal evangelism, even if effectively and fully launched from all present congregations, is totally inadequate to grapple with this major part of the unfinished task.

The Remaining World

Now, once we have recognized the existence of these three major groups, the remaining, or "other" non-Christians in Asia represent (by contrast) only a mopping-up operation. The astonishing novelty in Figure 4 is the large number of Christians culturally related to the remaining non-Christians. The number of Christians is of a totally different magnitude and proportion than in the previous diagrams.

Christians   Non-Christians

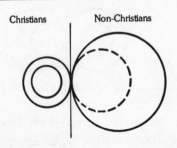

Figure 4. Other Asian Peoples

Who are the peoples in this catch-all group of "other" non-Christian Asians? There are, for example, 100 million Japanese. Are they all reachable by normal evangelism? Lest we exaggerate the number requiring cross-cultural evangelism, let us recall that while there are some fairly momentous cultural barriers to be crossed in the winning of all Japanese into the present variety of Japanese churches, such cultural barriers are in no way comparable to the barriers that prevent normal evangelism from even touching the vast bulk of the Hindus or the Muslims.

Thus the dotted circle—people who can (even conceivably) be reached by normal evangelism—is very much larger and includes not only many Japanese but also many Buddhists for whom there are in fact viable Christian traditions nearby that do not present a major social obstacle to their affiliation. In this estimate we are certainly not *over-* but *underestimating* the proportions of those who cannot be reached by normal (E-0 or E-1) evangelism.

Let us now move on to the last bloc of non-Christians outside of the Western world. We have already mentioned the non-Christian Muslims of Africa. This diagram shows the Africans who are neither Christian nor Muslim. Recalling that Africa was only 3% Christian in 1900, we stand amazed and pleased that the number of Christians is nearly equal to the number of non-Christians who are not Muslims! The number of committed Christians is large too.

Christians   Non-Christians

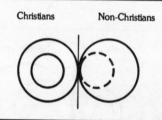

Figure 5. Other African Peoples

In view of these general contours for Asia and Africa, let us put them in a single chart and note the amazingly different proportions in the Western world. Figure 6 breaks the Western world down by isolating the population of the United States. Since these circles are drawn on the same scale as before, we see immediately that the Western world contains most of the nominal Christians. We can verify by eye that 85% of the nominal Christians are in the West while only a little over half of the committed Christians are in the West. It is even more obvious that the ratio of Christians to non-Christians is radically different in the Western world when compared to every area of Asia and Africa except non-Muslim Africa. Here then are the hard facts that maintain the credence of that long useful adage that where there are ten men at one end of a log and only one at the other, the priorities are obvious, especially if the ten men are at the smaller end of the log.

The Blunt Truth

To fully digest these diagrams can rightly absorb hours and hours of deep thought and earnest prayer. Here in scale drawing is the primary need in missionary strategy in the world today. Let us stop to recognize the following: (1) the great bulk of people on this planet are concentrated in Africa and Asia; (2) an even greater proportion of Africa and Asia (than the Western world) consists of peoples who do not consider themselves Christian; (3) the three largest cultural blocs of mankind—the Chinese, Hindus and Muslims—have only tiny Christian communities, if any at all, related to them; (4) in the case of China and India, only a very small proportion of the non-Christians are within normal evangelistic striking range of the existing Christians; and (5) despite the small number of Christians from within these large cultural traditions, their efforts to evangelize are mainly soaked up by the spiritual needs of the nominal belt that surrounds them.

Once we size up the need in these terms, it must be clear that *the only effective answer to the major part of this need can come from specialized cross-cultural organizations of the type represented by a standard mission society, either local or foreign.*

Since dealing with nominal Christians is the kind of evangelism most American Christians are acquainted with, it is not surprising that Americans who become involved in traditional foreign missions generally have a tough time figuring out how to do cross-cultural evangelism, and even if they do figure it out, have an even tougher time explaining to people back home how different pioneer missionary work is from the normal evangelism of cultural near-neighbors.

In these words I have no desire whatsoever to belittle the immensity of the commonly understood task of bringing about spiritual renewal among lifeless nominal Christians. This task of renewal is not only big, it is truly urgent, because worldwide outreach to non-Christians is considerably blunted by the scandalous behavior of nominal Christians back home in the Western world.

But the blunt truth is that if you had to guess at the proportion of all the evangelizing energies of evangelicals around the world expended on the renewing of nominal Christians you would probably come up with something like 97%. Yet, nominal Christians, though numerous, are only about one-fourth as numerous as the total of nominal Christians and non-Christians. Why should

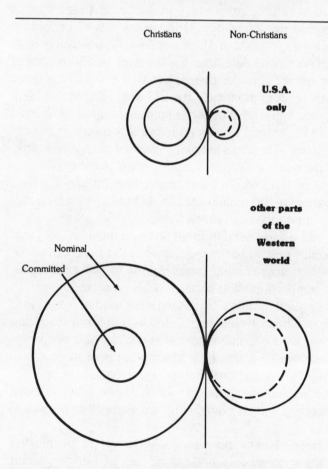

Numerical data from which these drawings are made is found in Table 1.

Figure 6. Western World (Europe, Russia, Americas, Australia, New Zealand)

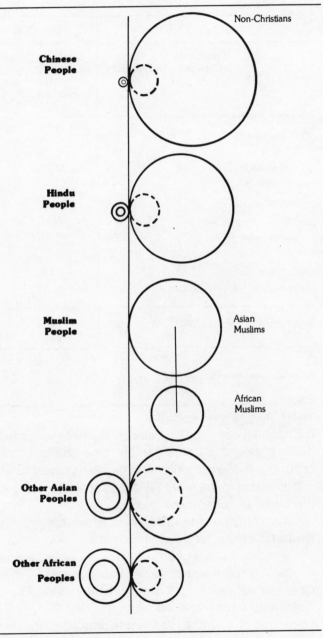

Figure 7. Non-Western World (Asia, Africa)

	Christians		Non-Christians		Totals
	Committed Christians	Nominal Christians	Reachable by ordinary E-1 Evangelism	Reachable only by E-2, E-3, Cross-Cultural Evangelism	
Western					
USA only 62	130	15	11	218
Other Western 68	738	173	142	1121
Non-Western World					
Chinese 2	1	38	803	844
Hindus 5	10	42	524	581
Muslims (Asia) .... .11	.05	15	434	449
(Africa) .... —	—	—	146	146
Other Asians 38	56	142	252	488
Other Africans 47	88	42	99	276
Totals 222	1023	467 (16%)	2411 (84%)	4123

All statistics are estimates for July 1977

Table 1. World Population (in millions)

the nominal one-fourth receive 97% of all evangelizing energies? Furthermore, it is incomparably more difficult to work cross-culturally: the larger job is also harder—unimaginably more diffi-cult in regard to the prerequisities of special training and prepara-tion required for any real success.

If we continue with missions as usual, that is, missions of the kind and of the scale in which we are now involved, there is simply no possibility of a major new thrust in missions. We must choose this day whether we will hide our eyes from the need and close our ears to the call or whether we will tackle with new de-cisiveness, mixed with humility and devotion, the unchanging command of a faithful God whose searching heart is still seeking. To hold back now will lead to misery, guilt and failure; the other choice leads through new open doors into the most spectacular mission challenge that any generation in human history has ever faced. If we will awake to new, daring obedience, the future is as bright as the promises of God.

Ralph D. Winter (Ph.D., Cornell) is the director of the United States Center for World Mission. This article is reprinted from The Grounds for a New Thrust in World Mission *by Ralph D. Winter (1977) by permission of the William Carey Library, P.O. Box 128-C, Pasadena, CA 91104. © 1977 by the Evangelical Foreign Missions Association.*

5

The Messenger's Qualifications

Isabelo Magalit

I was at Urbana 76. It was a most moving moment, when the call to commitment was made, to see half of the 17,000 people in this auditorium stand up, signifying their commitment to actively seek God's will concerning world evangelization.

"But the famous Urbana Convention is a joke!" said a veteran Western missionary to me shortly after I returned to Manila. "We have deceived these young people," he continued. "Where will these thousands of missionaries go? Where can they go? Who will accept them? When will Western, particularly North American, mission agencies wake up to the fact that their missionaries are simply not welcome in many parts of the world?"

Is my missionary friend, who is an American, right? Is the day of the Western missionary coming to an end? Is it time to say goodbye to the great Urbana missionary conventions? Shold the burden of making the gospel known to he ends of the earth now be shifted to the younger churches of the Third World?

No definitely no. World evangelism is the responsibility of the whole church, no less of the older churhes of Europe and America than of the younger churches of Asia, Africa and Latin America. And no more the responsibility of the one group than of the other. In fact, the dimensions of world evangelism are so awesome that only the whole church throughout the world, working in proper partnership, can get the task done. How to work together, as full partners, *that* is the question. It is a question that deserves plenty of attention, not the least in a misions convention such as Urbana. But no, the day of missions from the West is not over.

The time has certainly come for Western-based missions to give more careful consideration to the kind of missionaries they send. Of course missionaries from elsewhere need the same qualifications. Korean missionaries working in Bangkok need the same qualifications as American missionaries in Manila. But the precise outworking of the qualifications will differ somewhat. Today, I COME TO YOU AS A Filipino—a brother in Christ—speaking to North Americans who are eager to proclaim the Lord Jesus to all nations.

You must face up to the significance of your distinction— especially you who are Americans—that you come from the world's mightiest nation, which has implications for the missionary enterprise launched from your shores. The drama in Teheran does not detract from the greatness of your power. It illustrates it. The seizure of the U.S. embassy by Iranian students is an act of desperation—the wild swing of a little boy against what he regards as a bully. Yes, your political power has implications.

Your presence and your influence, your interests and your policies, your opinions and your goods—for example, Coke and Superman—are so ubiquitous around the globe that your missionaries cannot help being visible, easily identified as American.

You can affirm that identity unequivocally, without apology, sincerely believing that it stands for what is best in the world. Like one of your television preachers, you may even be convinced that "God loves America above all nations." Yes, you can proudly affirm your American identity.

Or, you can repudiate it in a valiant effort to make sharp the difference between American culture and the eternal gospel. We have all been sensitized to this issue of gospel and culture, particularly as it has been debated since the Lausanne Congress in 1974.

We do not ask you to choose between these two alternatives. The first one—pride in all that's American—happens frequently enough to be worrying, but I trust it is not the majority sentiment in this convention. The second, which is a denial of American culture, is not healthy for your dignity as persons and is probably impossible anyway.

There is a *third* way. What we are asking of you is to affirm what is positive in your being American and to be sensitive to what is negative. We trust that we are speaking the truth to you in love. Please listen to us because we are your brothers in Christ who greatly desire to be your partners in the worldwide mission of the church. Your mission is our mission, too.

What qualifications do messengers need if all nations are to obey and believe Jesus Christ? I suggest three essentials: First is zeal for God's glory. Second is love for needy people. And third is concern for the unity of the body.

Zeal for God's Glory

The first qualification for messengers is zeal for God's glory.

In Acts chapter 17, Dr. Luke tells us about the apostle Paul in Athens. Paul was waiting for Timothy to join him from Berea. While waiting in Athens, he looked around the city and was provoked as he saw that the place was full of idols. Provoked by idolatry! Dr. Luke uses a strong medical word: Paul had a paroxysm— his heart raced wildly within his breast as he saw the city's idols. He was full of righteous indignation from intense jealousy for the honor of the Lord Jesus. Promptly, he preached to the Athenians about Jesus and the resurrection.

Are you and I really convinced that God the Father has given to his Son Jesus the name Lord, the name which is higher than any othe rname, not only in this age but even in that which is to come (Eph. 1:21; Phil. 2:9-11)? Are we convinced that right now, the same Lord Jesus is seated at the Father's right hand—the place of highest honor and supreme authority? Do we believe that the Lord Jesus whom we serve is indeed the King of the whole universe? If so, like Paul we should be cut to the heart—suffer a paroxysm—whenever we contemplate the vast numbers of people who do not bow the knee to the Lord Jesus today. Think about it: some three billion people out of the world's four billion do not acknowledge Jesus as their Lord. Many of them do so because they have never properly heard of who Jesus is and of what he has done for them.

Such a vast multitude would rather worship their ancestors or a piece of wood or stone or some godless ideology or even the material goods of this world, rather than the Lord Jesus! This must drive us to greater zeal in sharing the good news.

"Woe is me if I do not preach the gospel" (1 Cor. 9:16)! For I deprive the Lord Jesus of the honor due his name. He alone is worthy of all "blessing and glory and wisdom and thanksgiving and honor and power and might" (Rev. 7:12). Evangelism is persuading men and women to recognize Jesus for who he is in order that they may bow before him and acknowledge him as Lord and Savior. Messengers of the evangel need more zeal for God's glory if all nations are to believe and obey the Lord Jesus.

But how often our zeal comes from mixed motives. Horatius Bonar (1808-1889), Scottish preacher and hymn writer, had a dream. He dreamt that the angels took his zeal and weighed it and told him it was excellent. It weighed up to 100 pounds, all that could be asked. He—in his dream—was very pleased at the result. But then the angels wished to analyze his zeal. They put it in a test tube and analyzed it in various ways, with this result:

14 parts were from selfishness
15 parts were due to sectarianism
22 parts from ambition
23 parts because of love for humanity, and
26 parts from love to God

Bonar woke up humbled at the thought, and dedicated himself anew.

Are we zealous for Christian service? We must be, for we are here. It must be missionary zeal that led us to this convention in the first place. But if our zeal were analyzed by the angels, what would be the results?

How much of our zeal comes simply from the American value system: the pioneering spirit that stakes out uncalimed territory, the rugged individualism that insists on doing one's own thing, the fierce competitiveness that delights in besting the competition? How much of our zeal would come from the party spirit? I am not only a flag-waving Filipino nationalist. I am also a Bible-believing Baptist and an Inter-Varsity partisan to boot! How much of our zeal comes from a desire to build a religious empire with headquarters in America and branches in a hundred nations? How much of our zeal comes from an emotional need to do something in order to feel useful?

What per cent of our zeal truly comes from a *burning* desire to promote the glory of God?

Genuine zeal for God's glory is costly, but it will cost us only our pride and our selfishness. God grant that we have less and less of both. Genuine zeal for God's glory can stand criticism—such as I have expressed—for criticism only serves to purify it, like fire purifies gold. Let the testing of our zeal produce purer motives, like gold, much fine gold.

My North American brothers and sisters in Christ, I ask you to send missionaries to the ends of the earth who are zealous for the glory of God alone.

Love for Needy People

The second essential qualification for messengers is love for needy people.

We live in a world of incredible human needs. Hundreds of millions of people are poor and hungry, homeless and illiterate, battered by illness and die young. From Vietnam, people are prepared to risk their lives to escape on rickety boats adrift at sea or live in overcrowded refugee camps with no facilities, to search for a better life. In our day we may be seeing the extinction of the people of Kampuchea, as both young and old die off because help that comes is too little and too late. There are many other examples elsewhere in the world of people in great need of the most basic necessities.

You come from the world's richest economy, the largest consumers of the world's goods and of its energy. Does the contrast mean anything to you?

James, the brother of the Lord, wrote these words to the early Christians:

This is pure and undefiled religion in the sight of our God and Father, to visit orphans and widows in their distress, and to keep oneself unstained by the world. . . . What use is it, my brethren, if a man says he has faith, but he has no works? Can that faith save him? If a brother or sister is without clothing and in need of daily food, and one of you says to them, "Go in peace, be warmed and be filled"; and yet you do not give them what is necessary for their body; what use is that? Even so faith, if it has no works, is dead, being by itself. (Jas. 1:27; 2:14-17)

Please do not send to us missionaries who insist on a dichotomy between evangelism and social concern. Missionaries who teach that evangelism is our main or even sole concern. Missionaries who say that ministry to the temporal needs of people will also be done, but only as we have time, and as our limited resources allow.

Such missionaries make it difficult for us to defend the gospel against the Marxist charge that Christians promise a pie in the sky for the by and by. That Christians who have links with the West are but tools of Western imperialism, perhaps innocent, but helping to perpetuate the pockets of privilege, leaving the wretched of the earth to remain wretched!

We must not simply react to Marxist criticism, even though I realize that for many of you Marxism is a theoretical question, while for us the Communist system is a live and attractive option. If it can feed the hungry millions, why not, why not? But we are not simply reacting to Marxist criticism. Rather, we must come to realize that unless our love is demonstrated in practical terms of helping to meet the need for daily bread, our gospel of love will eventually sound hollow and unconvincing.

Am I pleading for a return to the old social gospel? No, no. I myself trained as a medical doctor but abandoned the profession in order to become a preacher of the gospel. But I do ask you to resist

—to fight—every dichotomy between preaching the gospel of love and demonstrating that love for needy men and women through good works. It was General Booth, founder of the Salvation Army, commenting on James 1, who said: "We will wash it [our money] in the tears of the widows and orphans and lay it on the altar of humanity."

I have long admired the Salvation Army and their twin emphases on soup and salvation. They have much to teach us all. They follow the example of the Lord Jesus closely. For he who came to give his life for our redemption also fed the hungry, healed the sick and welcomed the outcasts of society. He is still our model. His mission is our mission.

I know that those who urge us to do evangelism only are fired by the urgency of the evangelistic task. I share their sense of urgency. In the words of the 1974 Lausanne Covenant: "More than 2,700 million people, which is more than two-thirds of mankind, have yet to be evangelized. . . . Missionaries should flow ever more freely from and to all six continents in a spirit of humble service. The goal should be, by all available means and at the earliest possible time, that every person will have the opportunity to hear, understand, and receive the good news."

Nevertheless, this section of the Covenant, entitled "The Urgency of the Evangelistic Task," goes on to say: "We cannot hope to attain this goal [of world evangelization] without sacrifice. All of us are shocked by the poverty of millions and disturbed by the injustices which cause it. Those of us who live in affluent circumstances accept our duty to develop a simple life-style in order to contribute more generously to both relief and evangelism."

Both relief and evangelism. We cannot, we *must* not divorce the urgency of the evangelistic task from our duty to help those in need of daily bread.

What does this mean for us today, to us gathered here to consider missionary service? It means facing the question: How can I, as a follower of the Lord Jesus, live more simply today in order to give more to help meet both the temporal and eternal needs of so many people on this planet? Some of you have had the opportunity to skip lunch in order to help feed the hungry. Praise the

Lord for such opportunities! However, let our act be more than a token undertaken only in missionary conventions, perhaps under considerable social pressure. Let our act be a sign of a commitment to a simpler lifestyle so that we can be more generous in sharing our goods.

Let me assure you, my brothers and sisters, that the question is no less demanding on me as it is on you. For I know large numbers of people who live on much less of this world's goods than I do.

Concern for the Unity of the Body

The third essential qualification for messengers is concern for the unity of the body.

In his great treatise on the church, Paul appealed to Christians to be "diligent to preserve the unity of the Spirit in the bond of peace" (Eph. 4:3)—not just to be willing to maintain the Spirit-given unity of believers, but to be eager to do so. It is a lovely picture word, *diligent* or *eager* (RSV). It means to spare no effort. The picture it brings to my mind is that of a miler setting the pace, at the head of the pack, doing the last lap. Coming to the last two hundred meters, he will pull out all the stops. It is time to give it all he has got! He will spare no effort.

Sadly, the missionary enterprise has not been noted for great effort in either maintaining or nurturing the unity of the body. R. Pierce Beaver, the well-known missions historian, was quoted in a paper given at the Lausanne Congress on World Evangelization as saying, "More and more I am convinced that exported divisiveness is the greatest hindrance to the spread of the gospel in the non-Christian world."

The church is a reality in nearly every place in the world where we want to send missionaries. We need to come to terms with her. We must be willing to recognize her as our partner. She may be financially poor, theologically unsophisticated and inefficient in her methods, but she is not our inferior. We cannot bypass her without sinning against the body. Paul reminds us that there is only *one* body (Eph. 4:4) with only one head, the Lord Jesus.

Ah, but someone says, some parts of the body are closer to the head. This person says that we have been given a grand vision for fulfilling the Great Commission, and we have the resources of the mightiest nation on earth for carrying it out. It is only sensible to conclude that the most efficient way to finish the job is to ask the rest of you to join us!

Perhaps we do not say these things. We only act this way. Our actions speak louder than our words: *West is best!* Is this simply bad theology or is it American pride?

One day, a Western missionary said to me in church: "Tomorrow we are sponsoring a youth march for Jesus in Plaza Miranda [downtown Manila]. Why don't you come and join us and bring your students along?"

"Well," I said, "I am not sure that that is the best way to demonstrate the reality of the gospel in this season of student demonstrations."

"Listen," she said to me, "can we ever work together? This division between us is diabolical."

I very nearly said to her, "Yankee, go home!" It was a struggle to keep back the words.

My North American brothers and sisters in Christ: Can we ever be partners? *Partners.* Why do you keep saying that you have a master plan for fulfilling the Great Commission and you want us to join you in carrying out your plans? Why can't you come to us and say: "I have come in obedience to the Great Commission. How can you and I fulfill it together?" Partnership means a fellowship of equals.

A true partnership, a fellowship of equals, is not impossible. Sitting down together, discussing a plan of action in mutual respect and confidence is not an idle dream. In June 1980, some 650 Christian leaders from all over the world met in Pattaya, Thailand, for the Consultation on World Evangelization (COWE). COWE, which is sponsored by the Lausanne Committee, is a good illustration of a fellowship of equals both in planning and execution. The COWE Director is David Howard from the United States. The Program Chairman is Saphir Athyal of India, and the Lausanne Committee Executive Secretary is Gottfried Osei-Mensah of Ghana.

COWE is by no means the only example. For those of you who are not very familiar with it, let me commend to you the International Fellowship of Evangelica Students (IFES). Fifty autonomous, indigenous national student movements have banded together to spread the gospel in the student world. Examine the IFES structure, its pattern of authority and decision making, its choice of leaders. We are not anti-American in IFES. Last July, we elected as Chairman of the Executive Committee to serve until 1983, Dr. John W. Alexander. The IFES is not perfect, but you will discover a fellowship of equals.

China, that great nation of one billion people—nearly a quarter of mankind—is slowly opening its doors. What will be our plan of action? Is everyone going to jump on the China bandwagon and insist once again on doing his own thing? Or shall we manifest concern for the unity of the body and ask ourselves: "What kind of action by outsiders will be best for the Church in China? How can we enter into partnership with the Church in China in order to advance the spread of the gospel?"

It is for the sake of the unevangelized millions that messengers need to be concerned for the unity of the body.

Have I been harsh? Have I caused you pain? I can only trust that our exercise tonight has been essential surgery. I pray that the Holy Spirit, the skilled surgeon, will apply the needed pain in a therapeutic way to help the body become healthier. So that the one body—you and I and the people of God across the world—may together proclaim to all nations that there is salvation in no one else, that there is no other name under heaven given among people by which we must be saved, except the name Jesus. Amen.

Isabelo Magalit is associate general secretary for the International Fellowship of Evangelical Students and general secretary of Inter-Varsity Christian Fellowship of the Philippines. This address was originally given at the Urbana 79 student missions convention and appeared in Believing and Obeying Jesus Christ, ©*1980 by Inter-Varsity Christian Fellowship of the U.S.A.*

6

That Amazing Thing Called the Church

Gordon MacDonald

If you really want to get serious about the matter of God's mission in the world, sooner or later you have to deal with the great fact of the church. If your heart is set on confronting people with the claims of Jesus Christ, leading to the possibility that they will choose to follow him, sooner or later you will have to deal with the great fact of the church. And if you are one of those who finds excitement in giving spiritual leadership to one or more believers so that they will grow in Christian maturity, sooner or later, you are going to have to deal with the great fact of the church.

This repetitive insight may leave a few people discomforted since it has been common recently for some Christians to pursue what might be called a churchless Christianity. And why not? Church has indeed been a joyless experience for more than one student. It is not unusual to hear the traditional liturgy of the anti-church man or woman who begins with the reasoning, "I was forced to go when a child," move on to "there was too much bickering and hypocrisy when I was a teen-ager" and conclude with a crescendo, "frankly, the church seems out of step with the world in which I live."

If I am familiar with these phrases, it is not so much that I have repeatedly heard them as much as the fact that I once employed them to describe my own attitudes toward the church and to justify why I found Sunday morning a choice occasion for catching up on what I thought was much-needed sleep. Besides, local Bible studies, leadership training groups and a host of friendships with other Christian students seemed to meet whatever need I had in the pursuit of corporate faith. So, I reasoned, the church was quite expendable.

Frankly, to think like that was bad theology and poor judgment on my part. I had some learning to do. I have to admit that the learning did not come easily either. The church in its congregational form does not always make it simple for one to come to positive conclusions about its importance in the scheme of eternal things. Here and there its history is sullied with some poor examples of the way things happen among the people called by God's name. And if one centers his or her attention on one or two local experiences in the past, or on a few generalizations often made about the irrelevancy of the church, it becomes easy to avoid confronting the issue of the church.

A serious study of the Scriptures on the question of God's program in the world became a shaking experience for me. What I discovered was a surprising continuity of principles which all pointed to the importance of my being heavily involved in the planting and maintenance of the church in its congregational form wherever God chose to place me. Among the principles which modified my earlier naive antithetical attitudes toward the church were these.

First, God has always had a "people." There has always been someone in the world with whom God chose to be in fellowship and through whom he would convey a redeeming message of love to those who would be willing to hear. In the earliest days of biblical history, the "people" were individuals such as Adam, Eve, Abel, Enoch, Noah and others. They shared a special insight into God's person and plan. It was not that they were better than anyone else, but they were presented with a responsibility which they generally accepted.

There followed a period of biblical history in which God spoke to *and* through a family—the extended family of Abraham. The twelveth chapter of Genesis enlarges this when God calls Abraham to leave his roots and embark upon a journey whose destination is unknown to him. Imbedded in the call is a challenge for Abraham to be a "blessing" to the world and the assurance that if he is obedient, his progeny will remain a "blessing" in the world.

That is exactly what happened. Abraham entered into a faith relationship with God, obeyed him, and was blessed in his old age with a son, Isaac. For a period of three generations God looked over the fortunes of this small group of people, protecting them, whispering into them new awarenesses of the meaning of worship and service.

Now some of those in Abraham's family—most notably Jacob —were not the finest specimens of holiness. There was duplicity, competition and outright crudity in some of their family relationships. But God persisted in his love for them, and they remained his people.

From the seed of Jacob came twelve sons who ultimately became the forebearers of the nation of Israel, a rather motley group of oppressed people who ended up living in Egypt for four hundred years. During those years, knowledge of the God of Abraham dwindled to almost nothing. What held them together primarily, beyond their racial affinity, was the oppression they were forced to endure at the hand of a succession of cruel Egyptian pharoahs.

But then there was that miraculous exodus, led by Moses, which drew them out from under oppression and to the foot of Mt. Sinai where they were once again reacquainted with their God. Among the very first things they were taught was something about their "peopleness." "If you will obey my voice and keep my covenant, you shall be my own possession among all peoples;

for all the earth is mine, and you shall be to me a kingdom of priests and a holy nation" (Ex. 19:5-6).

It must have been an awesome moment when this promise and challenge first sank into their spirits. These ragged and despised people were being called out by God to be priests and holy people. Later God would say to them, "you are the people of God," and that stamp upon them would mark their entire lives.

The story of the Old Testament is really nothing more than a description of the fortunes of the people of God, how they performed with brilliance on occasions and how they failed spectacularly on others. When they became ineffective in the later years through their resistance to God, he allowed them to face the consequences of their poor choices. The close of the Old Testament finds God's people struggling to come to grips with their specialness and their misuse of privileges given them.

I am convinced that Jesus Christ came partly to bring back to awareness the role and mission of the people of God. You could say he was the perfect "people." His sense of mission and his way of life plainly identified what he expected from men and women who wished to be God's people. An enormous amount of his time was taken up with the training of twelve men who, upon his ascension, became the founders of an enlarged dimension of the people of God, the church in Jerusalem, which quickly spread to other parts of the world.

Consider the plan the disciples-become-apostles implemented. Jesus gave them many commands on this before he left them to the power of the Holy Spirit. It is exciting to trace the growing awareness of these apostles, to see them discover that their mission was to preach the gospel *and* plant congregations. Evangelism was more than just leading people to Christ; it was bringing people into discipleship—and that meant relationship with one another as much as personal spiritual growth. Out of that emerged a further sense of mission as newly planted congregations moved out to plant still more congregations.

Later Peter would write of this incredible movement which melted Jews and Gentiles, rich and poor, slave and free, "You are a chosen race, a royal priesthood, a holy nation, God's own people, that you may declare the wonderful deeds of him who called you out of darkness into his marvelous light. Once you were no people but now you are God's people; once you had not received mercy but now you have received mercy" (1 Pet. 2:9-10).

Peter's statement is simply amazing. He has equated the church with the call given at Mt. Sinai centuries before. Obviously he sees the church right in line with the succession of relationships God has established through the years with individuals, families, a nation and now the church—the fullest, broadest form of redeemed humanity blessed with a mission, a relationship and heavenly privileges.

All of that makes one thing very clear to me. Being part of the church is being part of the people of God, and I need to understand both the privileges and responsibilities. I am part of an incredibly long and consistent chain of graciously called people.

Second, the church is a precious thing to God. When St. Paul was making his last visit in the area of Ephesus, he called a meeting with the leaders of the great congregation there. His agenda centered on the future of the church and its ongoing fidelity to matters of faith. In the midst of his talk with those spiritual leaders, Paul said this, "Take heed to yourselves and to all the flock, in which the Holy Spirit has made you overseers, to care for the church of God *which he obtained with the blood of his own Son*" (Acts 20:28).

Often we emphasize that Christ died for each of us as individuals. But I am astounded to hear Paul affirm that Christ died for the church. And here is the old apostle charging these congregational leaders with the importance of their maintenance of the church because it belongs to God, purchased by the blood of his own Son.

The first time I saw this, I was immediately rebuked for the number of times I had criticized the church and rebuffed it without realizing that God loved it even if it was like Jacob had been at times. Here Paul was placing a value upon the church, and the value was measured according to the blood of Jesus Christ. Could I dare to look at the church and see it any differently?

I was no less impressed when I discovered in Ephesians 4 that the Christ who had given his blood for the church then proceeded to give gifts to the church: apostles, prophets, evangelists, pastor-teachers. And add to that the further revelation that the Son of God makes intercession for the saints who are the church! It was a powerful message to me. How could I any longer miss the point that the church—being part of it, helping to plant it and fostering its ongoing health— was primarily where world mission was to be found?

Third, a part of the genius of the church is its universality. It took a while for the early church to both perceive and implement the notion, but the church, they discovered, was to become the most unique human organism in history. It was to include *every* possible human being who would name the name of Christ as Lord and Savior.

To be candid, there were some important folk who would like to have made the Pentecost incident a mere reformation in Judaism. They would like to have maintained a Jewish superiority in the church and relegated all others to a sort of second-class citizenship. After all, that had been their mindset for centuries, and it was part of what had ultimately rendered Israel ineffective as the people of God.

But the story of the book of Acts is that of the wedging open of the early believers to the genius of a universal church. Paul saw that genius when he would later write to the Galatians: "For as many of you as were baptized into Christ have put on Christ. There is neither Jew nor Greek, there is neither slave nor free, there is neither male nor female; for you are all one in Christ Jesus. And if you are Christ's, then you are Abraham's offspring, heirs according to promise" (Gal. 3:27-29). Incredible! The church is an organism designed to cut down all artificial human distinctions. There are to be no uniforms—such as proud Jewish religious personalities wore— that set people apart from one another. There is no gender, no racial affinity, no class structure which is carried into the church according to Paul.

I have never grown tired of seeing varied people worship together. A nine-year-old can worship sitting next to a ninety-year-old. There need be no discernible differentiation between a corporate president and a laborer laid off from the assembly line.

I have never grown tired of realizing that on the Lord's Day, the sun brings light each hour of its global migration to different congregations rise to sing God's praises. The earliest worship times belong to the believers of the Pacific, west of the international date line. If my geography is correct, the church in Indonesia joins in; then the Japanese and Philippine Christians. Then the underground churches of China and Southeast Asia. Siberian Christians get quickly into the act, joined by those in India and the few in Afghanistan. East Africa springs into motion as does the eastern European church. Then West Africa, the British, and soon after, the first of the Latin Americans. And finally, late in the holy day, the North American church enters the flow of praise that the rest of the believers in the world have been maintaining for almost eighteen hours.

God is hearing the universal church in the motion of worship. It has come from every age, culture, linguistic group and different form of expression. He is doubtlessly pleased.

Fourth, the congregation is the ideal environment for growth in spiritual maturity.

My wife, Gail, loves to grow plants indoors and outdoors. In her anxiety to see things grow, she has learned what makes growth possible. I have never seen her attempt to take a plant stem and stretch it like a piece of elastic. It would break of course. But she has learned to create an environment of growth which is a combination of temperature, moisture, sunlight and soil. When she achieves the delicate balance of all these things, the plant grows.

In what environment can a Christian achieve the most normal sort of growth? One in which there is the proper admixture of worship, fellowship, instruction and mission. The apostles orchestrated these very elements in the latter stages of Acts 2 when the Jerusalem congregation sprang into action. We also find them in Acts 11 when we read the description of that congregation at Antioch which commissioned the first foreign missionaries (see Acts 13).

Add to that environment the importance of mature leadership which can provide new Christians with fatherly and motherly wisdom and insight and you have an ideal atmosphere in which spiritual growth can take place.

Fifth, the church works effectively wherever Christians understand its purposes and make commitment to it. It is a fair statement to say that the apostles were deeply concerned that Christians commit themselves to the work of the congregation. The writer of Hebrews firmly directed people to worship regularly with one another so that we can provoke one another to grow.

Paul never gave up on shabby performances like that of the congregation at Corinth, but he begged people to heal their divisions and engender a deeper quality of servantlike love for one another. To the Thessalonians he made plain that submission to spiritual leaders was important. To the Philippians he suggested that the quality of their love for one another be an authenticating witness to the enemies of Christ and a warning to unbelievers that not to decide for the Savior would bring judgment. And writing to the Ephesians, it was the matter of mission: that through the church God was going to make known his grace and salvation.

The church, Paul is saying, is not an option for those of us who are Christians; it is our extended family; it is our team in mission; it is our prime relational identity. We are God's people, the church in the world. And we identify as followers of the faith when we join with other committed people of all generations and backgrounds to carry on its work.

Lastly, the church is the beginning and end of our world mission. It was a congregation which had the sense of the Holy Spirit to send out Saul (later Paul) and Barnabas. Having heard the call of the Holy Spirit (Acts 13:1-3), it recognized the uniqueness of the two men, sent them off, and later received them back for their report. A study of that congregation will make it plain that they were a group of believers hungry for teaching (Acts 11:26), compassionate in their caring for the whole person (Acts 11:28-30) and fervent in their worship (Acts 13:1-2). It is in such an atmosphere that a sense of world mission grows until it can be contained nò longer. A congregation sent out the first missionaries, and it cared for them when they returned.

Wherever the two men went, they tried to do one basic thing:

plant more churches. Why? Because they believed that congregations were the best expressions of the people of God, because they believed in that universal genius of how people are drawn together, because they saw the congregation as the environment for growth and because they anticipated that a congregation would regenerate itself.

As we gather for still another Urbana missions convention in 1981, among my many prayers is that in our pursuit of God's mission in the world we will rediscover something not fully appreciated by many young Christian students. And that is that our great mission is to plant the church in the world which in turn will give honor and praise to him who died for the church, and invested it with gifts so that he might present it to his heavenly Father as his most prized possession.

Gordon MacDonald is pastor of Grace Chapel in Lexington, Massachusetts.

Part II

The Messenger: Discipleship in Luke's Gospel

Yvonne Vinkemulder

Jesus first called people to be disciples—pupils, disciplined ones, learners. Then he called them to be apostles—sent ones. Before we can be sent with the good news, we must first learn. There is no better place than at the feet of the Master Teacher.

Luke carefully documents his account in an historical setting. You may wish to read through the entire book, noticing his emphasis on the kingdom of God, good news, prayer and the Holy Spirit. You can learn what kind of opposition Jesus faced, and how he met it. You can find how he prepared those he would send into the world with the good news treasure.

What will you need for these studies? First, a good study text in modern language. A paraphrase may help clear up an obscure point, but should not be used as a primary text. Second, if studying alone, you will also need a notebook to record main ideas and specific application. Third, bring an open mind to approach God's Word, ready for fresh perspective and new truth the Holy Spirit will give you. Lastly, be willing and eager to be corrected, instructed, trained in godliness—and to obey.

7

Foundations for Followers

Luke 6:12-49

Jesus' days were full, very full. He never traveled more than four miles an hour. Yet in three years he laid the foundations for a revolution that would span the world. Luke sandwiches the following account between two periods of heavy activity: teaching, miracles, opposition, crowds.

For Discussion
1. As you read Luke 6:12-49, try to compare Jesus' sense of priority with yours.
2. How did Jesus prepare to select a core of followers? Distinguish between *disciple* and *apostle*. [1]
3. Describe the scene as Jesus began to teach his disciples.
4. Contrast the two groups described in verses 20-26. Why is one's position happy and the other's lamentable?
5. Underline the verbs in verses 27-31. What principle here

should govern your behavior toward those hostile toward you? What examples does Jesus use to illustrate this principle?

6. What outstanding differences should there be between sinners and Jesus' disciples? What motivates a disciple to be different?

7. Mark the commands and their promises in verses 37-38. How do these expand what Jesus said before? Putting it all together, what kind of a person does he expect you to become?

8. What *basic* principles of discipleship does Jesus lay out in verses 39-49? From these, how would you distinguish a true disciple from a pseudofollower? What evidence is there that you are genuine?

9. Many would hear Jesus, and call him "Lord" (v. 46). Why are some stable and others unstable? How would you characterize yourself?

For Action

10. Glance back through these verses and isolate actions which require humility in a disciple. Which of these apply specifically to you? How will you apply Jesus' teaching on this today?

11. This passage is loaded with positive and negative opportunities to put Jesus' words into practice. Choose one specific command you will seek to obey today to strengthen your foundations. How, specifically, will you begin?

For Prayer

12. Thank God for the opportunity to hear and study his Word.

13. Ask God to show you attitudes and behavior changes that need to be uprooted if you are to be a "learner" and a "sent one." Then ask him to uproot these, and trust him to fill the vacuum and strengthen your foundations.

Note

[1]A disciple is a pupil, a follower, a learner. In Jesus' day it was common practice for a man to find a rabbi and stick closely to him for instruction. An apostle is a messenger; the word comes from the same Greek root which means to send or to send away.

8

Listen Up!

Luke 8:1-21

It's not what truth we know that counts; it's what we do with it! The Master Teacher first instructs his students, and then in four seemingly unrelated miracles (vv. 22-56) proves that he is worth listening to.

For Discussion

1. As you read Luke 8:1-21, notice first what Jesus says about listening. What makes a good listener?

2. Why does Jesus say he uses parables (v. 10)? Why do you think he reveals truth to some and obscures it from others?

3. Try to visualize, as his audience could, the setting for the first parable: a hand-tilled patch of land, a sower scattering the seed by flinging his hand out, the wind perhaps catching some of it. Using the chart on the next page, compare the four kinds of soil, what happens to the seed, and Jesus' interpretation.

4. How is listening like a growing plant; that is, what is necessary

	Soil	What Happened	Jesus' Interpretation
1			
2			
3			
4			

for the seed to sprout and produce? What is necessary for truth to sprout and produce? What do you think hinders God's truth from taking root in people?

5. What does all this say to us about evangelism? Can you detect how Jesus' ministry illustrates this principle (vv. 1-4)?

6. Jesus plants a very important principle in verses 16-18. Why do people light lamps? What is the point of this illustration?

7. Imagine yourself in the crowd, trying to listen, and a handful tries to squeeze through. Who were they, and what did they want? How did Jesus' response differ from what you would expect?

For Action

8. Summarize what Jesus says about hearing in this passage (about those who hear, understand and act, and about those who pay no attention). Using this as a basis, with whom do you identify most: Jesus' relatives, those he calls "family," or an anonymous member of the crowd? Explain.

9. There are two things we can do with God's truth: stifle and ignore it, or listen to it and obey. In two columns jot down times when you've done each. What has been the result produced by each?

For Prayer

10. Give thanks for God's truth, his Word: living, powerful and fruitful.

11. Confess disobedience and lack of faith which causes you to ignore his truth.

12. Ask him to help you understand, receive and practice the truth he has revealed to you. Specifically ask his help as you attempt to obey him today.

9

Teach Us to Pray

Luke 11:1-13

In small villages without shops, people would bake bread every morning. Hospitality was a sacred duty. So when an unexpected visitor arrived, the host would go to a neighbor to borrow bread. In the following passage, the neighbor, evidently a poor man living in a one-room house, was already asleep with his family. To get up would disturb everyone. But his friend is persistent. He will not go away; neither will he let his friend go back to sleep without giving him what he needs.

It has been said that there is no such thing as unanswered prayer, for each one receives a yes, a no or a wait. But for many of us, the problem is that we need to start in the kindergarten of prayer. "If we do not want what we are asking for enough to be persistent, we do not want it very much. It is not such tepid prayer that is answered."[1]

For Discussion

1. List your immediate prayer requests before you read Luke 11:1-13.

2. Why do you think the disciples asked Jesus to teach them to pray?[2]

3. In Eastern culture, a person's name was not just a convenient handle, but represented the whole person, the intrinsic character. What then would the phrase, "hallowed be your name" signify? How can you hallow the Father's name?

4. List the requests in Jesus' example (vv. 2-4). With what priorities and/or relationships is each concerned?

When you pray, where do you place your emphasis? Why?

5. What is Jesus' point in his illustration in verses 5-8? When you do not receive the answer you want right away, what do you tend to think and/or do?

6. Underscore the active verbs in verses 9-13. How is each one slightly different?

What is Jesus trying to teach?

7. What is the point of Jesus' comparison in verses 11-13? Why is what we know and believe about God important in prayer?[3]

8. What is the ultimate gift Jesus encourages the disciples to expect? When was this prayer to be answered (see Acts 1:12-14; 2:1-4)?

Consider the time and events intervening before the answer came. Why would a delay be beneficial?

9. Compare Luke 11:1-3 with Acts 1:14. How well had the disciples learned?

For Action

10. What do you learn about the relationship of teacher and disciple from this passage? If someone would say to you today, "Teach me to pray," how would you do it?

11. Compare your praying with Jesus' example. (Begin by categorizing the requests you listed at the beginning of the study.) With what are you most concerned? Are there some requests you would now scratch or change after this study? Other concerns you would add?

For Prayer
12. Categorize the things you've listed as your personal concerns for prayer under the following headings, and use this as a basis for prayer today and this week: God's Kingdom, Physical Needs, Relationships, Spiritual Concerns.

Notes
[1]Leon Morris, *The Gospel according to St. Luke* (Grand Rapids, Mich.: Eerdmans, 1979), p. 195.
[2]Consider that the Jewish (rabbinic) way of teaching was by demonstration; the Greek way by dissertation. It appears from the Gospels that Jewish teachers made much of public prayers; Jesus made much of private prayer. Notice how little time Jesus spends on content, and how much he spends on persistence.
[3]If a child asked for a stone or a snake when he needed food, do you think a parent would grant the request? What does this say about God's wisdom when we ask for the wrong things?

10

Keep Your Eye on the Goal

Luke 12:13-34

Jesus uses an unusual question as a launching pad to teach his disciples some very basic truths about misplaced affection. Anything which holds us back from pursuing his goal—the kingdom—is sin. He spots two opposing dangers: being possessed by too much (greed), and fear that we will not have enough (anxiety). Both stem from the same root: independently believing we can control our circumstances rather than recognizing God's gracious gifts and trusting the heavenly Father to "give us our daily bread."

Jewish laws of succession decided most questions of dividing an inheritance, but when there was doubt, the aid of a rabbi was sought to settle any disputes as to the law. So this man came to the best rabbi he could find. But Jesus came to preach good news not to settle petty disputes!

For Discussion

1. Read Luke 12:13-34. From the man's specific request, what can you surmise about the dispute and how he would like it settled?

2. Looking at Jesus' answer, what danger did he see? Why is it a particular threat?

3. Contrast the preoccupation of the man in the parable (vv. 16-21) with the ideal Jesus sets forth in verses 32-34. Why is the rich man's solution foolish?

4. Why is it unnecessary to *worry* about physical and material needs?

5. Contrast the goals of citizens of the world with goals of citizens of the kingdom (note v. 30).

6. Why are anxiety and faith incompatible?

7. What does Jesus promise to those who put God's kingdom ahead of their own? To what do "these things" refer? How can you seek his kingdom?

8. How does verse 32 expand your view of God's design for you? How can this help you overcome anxiety and loosen your grip on possessions?

For Action

9. Quickly jot down the major activities and pursuits you've been engaged in this week. What do these show about your affection and treasure?

10. From these verses, can you pinpoint any way in which you are tempted to misuse God's good gifts to you? What step might you take today to trust his resources instead of your own?

Your Prayer

11. Thank God for the abundance of gifts he has given to you, including material things.

12. Confess any tendencies to anxiety or greed, or other misuses of his gifts.

13. Commit yourself and all he has given you to the single goal: to put his kingdom and his righteousness first.

Yvonne Vinkemulder is the director of development for Inter-Varsity Christian Fellowship of the U.S.A.

Part III

The Urbana Convention

This part helps you think about yourself and your preparation for Urbana—or any other mission experience.

Robert Oerter, Jr. *talks to you about your attitude toward the will of God. Don't miss this one!*

Michael Evans-Layng *gives you pointers on how to prepare for Urbana.*

William J. Treguboff *gives tips on getting the most out of the total Urbana experience.*

Pete Hammond *offers some practical helps for believing God and heading off problems at Urbana.*

Ken Shingledecker and James Rutz *provide hints on how to talk to mission agencies at the convention.*

11

Undebatable Guidance

Robert Oerter, Jr.

Many students are honestly perplexed when they try to answer the question, "What is God's will?" It's a problem for all of us.

Facing divergent paths, we simply are not sure which one to choose. So we waver uncertainly at the crossroads. If we had a clear wind of divine direction, we would snap to attention and obey with joy. At least we think we would.

When the Word of God does not speak clearly about a problem we face, we must responsibly seek God's will for that particular moment of action. Searching for God's open door, we must sift facts, learn from spiritually-minded counselors, pray with openness of mind, dedicate ourselves to obey. Often Christians try to escape a responsible search for God's will by leaning on the judgments of others or by mechanically handling a "chance" passage of Scripture.

Such irresponsible shortcuts may bring action and relief, but they will not bring the peace of discernment based on honest inquiry and responsible action. Most of us at sometime or other have longed for the quick, neat formula, the easily followed rule of thumb, the overwhelming bolt from the blue. But God normally does not reveal his will in these ways.

The Test of Obedience

To test our willingness to follow God *if* his will were known, let's consider obedience where God's will *is* known. Certainly for the earnest Christian, God's known will is not debatable. Once his will is clear, our will should be responsive. We then don't quibble, argue, extenuate or delay. We obey because we have received undebatable guidance from our Lord.

Surprisingly, much of God's guidance is easy to discern. It is unclouded by mystery or uncertainty. God has spoken about some things in his Word, and no further revelation is necessary. You don't stand in perplexity and ask, "Is this right for me or is this wrong?" You don't engage in a moral tug-of-war because God has removed the necessity for conflict on this particular issue. He has given you undebatable guidance.

A clear instance of such firm, undebatable guidance is seen in the Ten Commandments. This moral law of God has not been abrogated. The fabric of the universe is still moral, and God shows no indication of accommodating to lower goals by reducing the validity of his moral law. This revelation of God's will is not really debatable, and we must accept it as valid, personal guidance for ourselves today. This law confronts us with the challenge of a normative will of God; it is a plumb line to judge our lives if they are out of line. These commandments search us in depth and touch every basic relationship of our lives. Therefore, the Christian doesn't say, "I wonder if I ought to cheat in this exam. I didn't get a chance to prepare very well, and I wonder if the Lord would understand my situation." You don't need guidance at this point. You don't *need* to ponder God's will. He has already said, "Thou shalt not steal."

And God has given similar guidance on scores of other matters.

We ought to know God's Word so well that we readily sense his reaction to our daily choices. As committed people we should seek to view all our life from the divine perspective. Oswald Chambers has said that we should discern the "goings" of God. He means that we ought to know how God thinks, how he goes about things. The goings of God are the habits of God, the characteristic reactions of God, the ways of the Almighty.

If we learn to obey God where his will is obvious, we'll develop the ability to sense his will where the specific Word is not so obvious. The more we live in joyful obedience to the best Lord, the more we'll discern his likes and dislikes.

On Presenting, Squeezing and Renewing

Consider Romans 12:1-2: "I appeal to you therefore, brethren, by the mercies of God, to present your bodies as a living sacrifice, holy and acceptable to God, which is your spiritual worship. Do not be conformed to this world but be transformed by the renewal of your mind, that you may prove what is the will of God, what is good and acceptable and perfect." Here we see three principles for knowing God's will.

First, present your body to God. Present yourself to God, not in some theoretical, moody, abstract, bloodless commitment, but present yourself tangibly to God. Give your body, yourself, to God. The only place where Christian character is formed is in the body of a Christian. It is in our bodies that we show the reality of our commitment to our Lord. Convincing Christianity affects our bodies. If our Christianity does not get to our bodies in demonstrable grace of action, our religion is humbug. Professing lips and lying feet betray the compromise of our response. We haven't yet yielded our bodies. Much of God's guidance eludes us because we have evaded the totality of this first principle: present your body to the Lord.

Second, do not let the world squeeze you into its mold. Don't feel that you must succumb to the insistent pressures from the outside, subtle or obvious. The patterns of a passing world are not authentic guidance for a pilgrim people. Some of the patterns of our culture are helpful, good, even beauty touched, buy many of them are not. Many beckoning voices are anti-Christian. Many earnest forces are sub-Christian. Don't let the world scheme, which leaves out the judging mercy of the living God, govern your life. Don't let the world squeeze you into its mold.

Third, be renewed by the Holy Spirit. Willingly yield to God. Steadfastly resist unworthy pressures. Then daily, habitually, open your inner life to the dynamic renewal of God's Holy Spirit. Seek his clean control of your growing life. Let God make you inwardly fresh for each day's responsible living, " . . . strengthened with might through his Spirit in the inner man, and that Christ may dwell in your hearts." If these three principles are personal realities in your being, discernment of your Lord's will is sure to follow.

The Search Is On

In my own wrestling with the will of God, I have seen several important truths.

1. If you have missed God's ideal will for your life, don't panic or despair. Receive his forgiveness through Christ and set your heart to know and do his will where you now find yourself.

2. Failures are to learn from. Worse than failure, losing heart keeps you from a courageous, new beginning with a pardoning Lord. Failures aren't to cripple us; failures are to learn from.

3. Take care of your present task. Your future status will take care of itself.

4. Let God engineer your sphere of service as you obey him. The sphere of service is not nearly so important as the quality of your obedience.

5. It is useless to search for God's will if you are unwilling to obey. Often we waste our time in an agony of searching. We kid ourselves. But we do not kid God who knows that we really don't intend to obey. We flirt with unfruitful deviations from God's will and finally succumb to disobedience.

To search for God's will, we must be willing to obey.

Robert Oerter, Jr. is pastor of the First Presbyterian Church of Boulder, Colorado. This article first appeared in HIS magazine.
© *1962 by Inter-Varsity Christian Fellowship of the U.S.A.*

12

Before You Go:
Getting Ready for Urbana

Michael Evans-Layng

Overwhelmed.

Never in my life had I been with 14,000 people for a week of intense learning. Never had I been so dramatically faced with the needs of our broken world and God's strategy for meeting those needs. Never had I been exposed to so many people from so many diverse backgrounds who were zeroed in on one thing: trying to understand what Jesus their Lord wanted them to do so that they could go out and do it.

What was the Urbana 73 missions convention for me? I was a junior at the University of California at San Diego when I attended that, my first, Urbana. I'll not forget it: four days packed with experiences, sensations and information that changed my life in fundamental ways. To sum up what I gained, I might use the word *perspective* or perhaps *window*. I gained a new window on the world, a look at things—including myself—from God's perspective.

Hearing so much about the world's needs and about the lordship of Christ added up, strange as it may seem, not to a feeling of despair but to one of hope! I saw clearly for the first time that as acute as the world's needs are, our Lord is ready, willing and able to deal with them because he *is* Lord. I saw that his lordship does not make him some big Cosmic Scrooge, as Paul Little said, out to ruin everyone's fun. He is our hope and he has a spot somewhere for *me* in the grand scheme of things. Amazing!

Yet my feelings of being overwhelmed were not all positive. It was terribly easy to lose sight of that budding perspective he was building in the midst of all the seminars, the snow, the talks and the *people!* Getting ready for these things before coming to Urbana can help maximize the positive while you're there and allow the Urbana experience to have more impact in the long run. Preparing adequately is also an exercise in good stewardship of time, energy and money. Believe me. I've been there. Without some discipline it is all too easy for your resources to be needlessly squandered at a conference of the size and scope of an Urbana.

How can you prepare? If God wants you to go to Urbana, prayer is the place to start finding that out. If he does want you to attend, you can also count on the fact that he wants to use the convention to communicate some important things to you about himself, the world and you. Prayer *before* you plunge into all the hubbub will help you hear his voice *during* the hubbub. No less important, it will help you to be receptive to what he is driving at.

Having a prayer partner for all of this wouldn't be a bad idea either. Find someone to pray with (maybe weekly) about why you are going. If you want to go just because so many others are or to please your pastor or to get a spiritual shot in the arm, your motives need some work. Pray that you'll go because God wants you there. Pray about the financial need. Pray about your openness to learn once you're there. And don't forget to pray for the convention itself.

Second, read. Read carefully through this book. Get into a small group that will go through these articles and the Bible studies. If you can't find one, you might think about starting one. And if you're a bookish sort of person, you might want to tackle

Christian Mission in the Modern World by John Stott or (for the less ambitious) the booklets *You and God's Work Overseas* and *Say Yes to Mission* (all from IVP). If you're really brave, try a missionary biography. You might be surprised at what you find.

Third, I would encourage you to find a missionary and ask him or her some questions. For instance, "How did you know that God was calling you to the mission field? How did you prepare? What is your personal vision for the work you're involved in? How do you spend your time on the field? Off the field?" Also ask his or her opinion on some of the current issues in the world of missions. "How do you respond, and why, to the call from some church leaders in the Third World for a moratorium on sending missionaries from the West? What do you think about self-supporting missionaries vs. missionaries sent from a mission board and financially supported by people from their home country? How do you feel about the Church Growth people and their call for evangelizing within homogeneous cultural groups?"

Fourth, consider using multimedia tools from TWENTYONE-HUNDRED Productions for your church or campus group. A variety of shows are available to widen your view of the world and the challenge to reach it. A creative and entertaining way to inform and motivate. Rental information is available from TWENTYONE-HUNDRED Productions, 233 Langdon, Madison, WI 53703.

Fifth, be sure to bring a checkbook or some extra cash for the offering that will be taken for student work overseas and to purchase books that will be available in the Armory.

Finally, come as rested as possible. Don't plan other draining events into your calendar for the two weeks preceding the convention. Get lots of sleep. You may have finals and Christmas activities to contend with, but realize that Urbana is very intense physically and emotionally. You need to be in shape to run the good race.

Have a good time preparing for Urbana! It is my prayerful desire that you will be sensitive to God's will not only concerning Urbana but also concerning the larger matter of your life as a whole.

Michael Evans-Layng is a staff member with Inter-Varsity Christian Fellowship in California.

13

Once You're There: Making the Most of Urbana

William J. Treguboff

Urbana is a total experience—physically, emotionally, intellectually, spiritually. It is exhilarating and draining in each of these ways. There are a few practical things you can do to make sure the drain doesn't overwhelm the exhil.

Take emotions, for example. You know—love, hate, fear and the boys. Well, one of the drain-type emotions possible at Urbana is lostness. With 17,000 of them and one of you, it's understandable. Of course the way to combat lostness is with companionship which can help produce security. (That's an exhil-type emotion, by the way.) And right in the convention schedule are ways to get companionship. Each morning you will meet for a small group Bible study with about nine other people from your living unit. Each evening you will meet again with the same people for a time of sharing and prayer. This small group will become a crucial part of your Urbana experience as it gives you an opportunity to talk about what you are hearing, thinking and feeling with a few people who are experiencing the same things. The members of your small group can become your best friends at Urbana.

Then there's a little trickier drain-type experience you're likely to meet up with. It's the I've-been-standing-in-line-a-long-time-and-my-feet-hurt-and-this-is-frustrating emotional/physical combination drain. You could be experiencing this the first day at registration or anytime during the week while waiting for a meal or while trying to get into a special workshop. Yet here's a chance to get to know a couple of new people, to exchange ideas, or perhaps to help someone who has other problems besides sore feet.

Not to bypass the gray-matter side of things, the topic of the convention is missions, and your brain will be challenged from many different angles. Read the program schedule carefully sometime during your first twenty-four hours. Set some priorities of things not to be missed. Get a grasp of the structure of events. If confusion or questions arise, seek out an Inter-Varsity staff member or your small group leader. Take time to pray too, to give your mind a rest before God. Allow him to bring a calm so you can focus your mind and heart once again.

You can make Urbana a visual experience in ways besides viewing the multimedia shows. Locate by sight some of the prominent landmarks of this large University of Illinois campus—the Assembly Hall, Huff Gym, the Armory. Then find them on the campus map in your convention program which you receive at registration. Locate your living unit and your designated dining area as you move about the campus with reference to the other recognized landmarks. (Doing this can also help prevent the feelings of lostness I spoke of earlier.)

The weather at an Urbana convention can be quite cold—sometimes temperatures can fall below zero, accompanied by a side order of snow and wind. For people unaccustomed to cold or severe weather this can be somewhat of a shock. If you are not familiar with and accustomed to a midwestern winter, talk to people who know what ice and snow are like. Ski enthusiasts might offer suggestions for what is advisable and practical for potential Urbana weather. Aim for clothing that will provide you with warmth (layers of clothes, not one big coat), mobility and comfort, rather than exotic paraphernalia.

When all is said and done, Urbana is mostly a matter of attitude: a willingness to rish your self in a new and unique setting, an act of commitment to God beforehand, an attitude of initiative in becoming familiar with a program and a schedule, and a spirit of inquiry about surroundings, people and events. Are you surprised that these attitudes are the same ones needed by a missionary experiencing the uniqueness of a culture for the first time? Your attitude and tactics in relating to surroundings, people, geography and weather can in itself be a parable of a missionary experience.

May God be with you as you stride across campus, as you sit in the Assembly Hall, as you stand in line, as you chat and pray with people, and as you hear his voice and experience his love during that week.

William J. Treguboff, formerly on staff with Inter-Varsity Christian Fellowship, is currently working towards a Marriage and Family Counseling License in California.

14

Hints for Handling an Abnormal Blessing

Pete Hammond

I have attended six Urbana gatherings and numerous other conferences for believers. They can be a blessing or a blight. It is not a normal experience to gather with so many of God's children this side of heaven. As good stewards we need to take special measures to honor the privileges. Here are some hints.

Believe God:
☐ to guide you by careful study of the schedule before you get to Urbana and then daily during the convention. Note that the focus of each day's major meetings is as follows: Day 1—Christ's Message; Day 2—Christ's World; Day 3—Christ's Missionary; Day 4—Christ's Lordship.
☐ to fill your life with new friends at meals, in your Bible study group, and while traveling together. Decide now to get to know them and to share yourself with them.
☐ to change and broaden your thinking about yourself, your

career and your values. Think hard about your future. Write down your reactions each day and share them with your prayer group. Think them through when you get home, too.

☐ to equip you to help students from your school who could not attend, relatives back home, your home church when you return. In other words, look at yourself as attending for the sake of others. Get materials they can use too. Pray daily for them.

☐ to use your INTERCRISTO print-out to help sort out lots of good information about ministry, mission agencies and opportunities. (See more in the next article.) Go to the Armory the first day just for orientation, then seek out key connections the following days.

Oppose the World, the Flesh and the Devil:

☐ by eating decently—that is at least two good, slow meals a day while at Urbana and during travel. Drink lots of fluids. The heated buildings tend to dehydrate you.

☐ by sleeping each night. Sleep *is* spiritual.

☐ by spending a time alone with God each day praying, meditating in Scripture (using the material that will be provided) and thinking through the day.

☐ by sharing your needs, reactions and questions freely with a prayer partner and your Bible study/prayer group.

☐ by asking hard questions gently of yourself, friends, speakers and, especially, the missionaries.

☐ by being sensitive to others and seeking to understand those who are insensitive or offensive. Seek help from your small group leader or one of the staff if you need it.

☐ by pacing yourself through all the meetings, taking notes of key ideas and then buying the compendium for review and sharing with others.

This is probably the largest temporary family you'll ever be a part of. Rejoice in the riches, respond gently to the differences, and praise God together.

Pete Hammond is director of specialized ministries for Inter-Varsity Christian Fellowship of the U.S.A.

15

Talking with Mission Agencies

Ken Shingledecker and James Rutz

Each afternoon at Urbana you will have the opportunity to interact with representatives from more than 130 mission agencies. These representatives will be at mission displays in a massive building known as the Armory. Now, if you know what agencies you want to talk with and what questions you want to ask, your visit to the Armory can be very helpful. But if like most students, you do not have any idea what to ask or which to visit, you could find the crowded Armory just one exhausting experience. How can you avoid that?

First, when you register at Urbana you will be given a computer print-out produced in INTERCRISTO. This print-out will list about ten mission agencies whose displays you should visit. These agencies are determined by matching your abilities and interests (as indicated on your Urbana registration form) with the opportunities that mission agencies have available. You should use this print-out as your personal guide to the Armory.

Second, all of the mission-agency displays will be laid out in rows in the center of the Armory. The displays will be in alphabetical order starting from the northwest corner. Graduate-school displays will be toward the east end of the Armory.

Third, do not be intimidated by the large crowds around each display. If you cannot talk to an agency, visit some of the surrounding displays and then try again. Or you may want to attend some of the elective seminars or go take a nap and return to the Armory when it is less crowded. Crowds are usually thinner right when the Armory opens each afternoon and on the second and third full days of the convention.

Fourth, do not feel compelled to attack the Armory every afternoon of the convention. Plan your time so that you can avoid it altogether on one or more days. Try to meet with friends in some building other than the Armory so you do not have to fight the crowd. This will also make the crowd smaller for those who must go to the Armory.

Fifth, here are some tips on what information to seek from each agency.

Statement of Faith   Although most nondenominational boards are conservative, they are not highly detailed in their doctrinal statements. Because of this, you will probably have little trouble agreeing with them on the basics if your theology is conservative. Further, you may be surprised to find that some denominations with a liberal membership have a missionary force that is quite conservative.

Countries   Most missionary candidates have at least some feelings of preference for a certain field or area or type of subculture. But try not to be overly rigid because many boards will want to make strong suggestions about your location. Long experience shows that God often speaks to a candidate through a board!

Track Record   How well is the agency doing? What has been its impact on the field? Has the work grown, especially in the last two years? Even though work is very slow in some countries, a board should have *something* to point to.

Size   On the positive side, a small board has the advantages of a friendly, informal family. A large board has the fringe benefits of a solid, sophisticated organization. On the negative side, the sloppy methods of some small boards have helped to keep them small for decades. And the bureaucratic efficiency of some large boards could give you that lost feeling of being merely a cog in a big machine.

Importance   How needed is the board? What would happen to the progress of world evangelization if it disappeared? Just how much is riding on its success? Remember that some of the less dramatic types of work (for example, teaching missionaries' children) are in the background but nonetheless essential.

Goals and Management   Is the board moving in a clear direction? Do the directors actually help their people? It's difficult to tell just from publicity material; a dedicated field staff with all eyes on the Lord may stumble and flounder from one huge success to another for years, even though supervisory support is erratic.

Type of Work   Does the board actually need you? If you feel you should get into one particular type of work, make sure they want people in that line now! If you're more flexible, no problem.

Leadership   Who are the leaders, the guiding lights? How long have they been with the board? What is their reputation in the church? Don't be bashful about asking people from other boards about their leadership. You aren't digging up dirt; you're doing your homework wisely.

Organization   Is the board appointed? Elected? Is the whole show run by one man? Is it run as an oligarchy by one family? (Some fine small boards are.) And are they authoritarian, democratic or somewhere in between? Is the individual missionary's voice heard in policy discussions? What is their attitude toward women?

Origin   How and when did they get their start? As a natural outgrowth of the ministry of one person or small group? As a splinter from another board? As a new outreach by an established organization?

Standards   What qualities and qualifications must you have as a candidate? Does the board provide (or require) special training? The rule of thumb here is to seek out a board whose standards you just barely meet. Then you will be in the most outstanding organization that you could qualify for.

Turnover How many years does the average missionary stay on? And where do they go after they leave—into some other notable work or into thin air?

Personnel Sources Where do the candidates come from? One denomination? Several countries? The white-collar culture? If you were reared in the Oakland ghetto you may be broadened by working alongside exfarmhands from Missouri, but be prepared for a few adjustments.

Finances What if you're in the Upper Amazon Valley and your support drops off one month? Is this board's financial policy sound? Is it open to the public? Are their contributors solidly behind them with a high per-person support figure? Is their overhead expense less than a quarter of the total budget?

Style Finally, there is that indefinable business of *feel*. Are these your kind of people? If not, do you like them anyway? Are you comfortable with them? Talk with missionaries on furlough. Write to someone on the field in the country which interests you. Visit the field if you can. It's worth the effort; it's like picking out a new family.

Don't ever let yourself get bogged down, though, in the details of choosing a board. Remember, if God has called you to the field, then someone is waiting for you and will be hurting if you don't get there.

Ken Shingledecker is on loan from IVCF-USA to Daystar Communications in Nairobi, Kenya. James Rutz is director of communications of Chuck Colson's Prison Fellowship ministry in Washington, D.C. He wrote the last half of this article which originally appeared in the March 1980 issue of HIS magazine under the title "Check List for Missions." © 1980 by Inter-Varsity Christian Fellowship of the U.S.A.

Part IV

What's Next?

What can you do after learning so much about missions?
Russell Weatherspoon has a few suggestions for
getting ready now for what God might have in mind for then.
Ruth Siemens helps you raise your world consciousness.
Ned Hale gives you lots of how-to's for getting involved
with international students.
Melvin J. Friesen happens to think everyone is
called to help in Christ's global mission.
Lastly there is a sheet to help you sum up how you
understand your role in that mission.

16

Cultivating That Anywhere Spirit

Russell Weatherspoon

After an experience like the Urbana Missions Convention, perhaps the first reaction of some would be to find a global map, look for the spot diametrically opposed to our hometown and, Urbana memorabilia and all, head for it. Now, folks who do this might encounter difficulties, not the least of them being that the charted spot might be in the middle of an ocean—in fact, there might not be any land, just ocean. But I understand the sentiment: "Strike while the iron is hot!"

Preparing to Serve

We should have realized by now that a prerequisite for missions is a desire to see others introduced to the Lord Jesus, that part of being a missionary is the giving of our professional or vocational abilities to the country in which we are serving. Let us suppose that you have little desire and few abilities. What is to be done?

Well, if you are willing to give yourself to your studies, by the time you graduate you will have gained something to give vocationally. That problem is solved. In other words, a little less moonlight and a little more lamplight.

However, vocational ability alone will not enable you or prepare you to be a missionary. You need to develop a strong desire to share the gospel. A weak desire can in reality be an admission that you never have had the opportunity to learn how. Both your campus fellowship and your local church can be minischools of missionary training. Through activities such as evangelistic Bible studies, booktables and special presentations, you can learn to talk to and exchange ideas with strangers. Over a period of time you will watch some of those strangers become friends and some of those friends become Christians. Your campus group could also help you get acquainted with foreign students.

At Brooklyn College in New York one experience holds my memory's attention with a tighter grip than all the rest. During a special presentation, which our Inter-Varsity chapter inoffensively called "Repent," an Oriental girl wandered in. She was a student of the martial arts and of Confucian philosophy. She managed to get the name of our group, its general purposes and the fact that we have a booktable once a week. From that initial encounter blossomed a dialog and a relationship between this young lady and our club unparalleled in the experience of many of us. After about a year spent mostly in questioning us, visiting our meetings and requestioning us, she gave her life to Christ. I know there are many of you who have had similar experiences. The thrill of watching someone who is earnestly searching for truth and who then finds it in Jesus Christ through the leading of the Holy Spirit is nothing less than exciting. If there is no formal fellowship of believers on your campus, why not start one?

A second source of training and experience is a local church which can help cultivate in you the spirit of cooperation and obedience as you assume responsibilities delegated to you by the leadership. In any fellowship, willingness to serve is desirable, but on the mission field it is indispensable.

You'll also want to take time to write to some mission boards.

Get to know them. What are their present personnel needs? What is their financial status? What do they consider major goals in the operation of their mission? How do the people where they minister receive them? What do they require educationally, medically and doctrinally of their candidates for the field? How much support will you personally be responsible to raise?

During most of my college life I worked with High School Evangelism Fellowship, an organization which trains Christian young people to evangelize their high schools. Helping the students memorize Scripture and teaching principles of witness was fun. I was soon confronted, however, with the ominous task of raising my support, which, in my mind—although I knew really nothing about it—meant walking from church to church with a cup outstretched, a pitiful look on my face and the hope in my heart that some born-again person would have pity on me. The reality of the situation was totally other: I found that both churches and individual believers took an interest in what I was doing and requested the privilege to give. I soon learned that this was a method, and a biblical one, of inviting others in on the blessing of God. (Paul describes it in Phil. 4:10-19.) In short, if you have never raised support and are nervous about it, don't be.

Combating Racism and Ethnocentrism

There's a lot of talk these days in missions about racism and ethnocentrism. We are living in a country which is racist. Racism thrives on ignorance. So does ethnocentrism. What are we going to do? I have an idea. It might not work, but I have an idea. How about if some of you folks from the rural towns beat it over to the suburbs this summer and take orders from somebody in a local church there and learn what it's like to live in the suburbs. How about you folks from the suburbs beating your way over to the urban areas and taking orders from a local church there. How about some of you people from urban areas beating your way to a rural section. Mess with the cows and the pigs for a while. I think this will prepare you if not for the foreign field at least to understand that the way you do things is not the only way people do them.

A fellow came from a hick town in New Jersey to New York City. Like many nice white folk that come from hick towns to bust open the deep, dark cities in which I live, he came with his crew cut, his smile and his gimmicks, which definitely work out in the suburbs but sometimes don't work in the cities. Nevertheless, he came. He had his rural ways about him, and he had his ethno-centrism about him, and to some slight degree he had his racism about him. And he was my Inter-Varsity staff leader.

But in those days of 1964 to 1967, as I watched on television things like Selma, Alabama, George Wallace and Lester Maddox, as I watched a part of America tell me they still did not consider me a man and as I tried to figure out whether Christianity was part of that statement—whether Christianity was telling me I was not a man, I was not even a person—here was a hick whose life was controlled by the Lord Jesus Christ. As far as I was concerned, and as far as many of the kids of my neighborhood were con-cerned, he was naive. But we all knew he was controlled by the lordship of Christ.

If you come from a city and God has commanded you to go to a rural area, go. If you come from a rural area and God has com-manded you to go to the suburbs or anyplace else, go. Don't try to be a city slicker if you're a hick. And if you're a city slicker, don't try to be a hick. Just go and learn. Elisabeth Elliot says that for a whole year while she was among the Aucas,

I watched and learned and kept my mouth shut. I had to keep my mouth shut most of the time because I did not know the Auca language. For once I listened and had nothing to say. It was a valuable exercise, and although the language itself was highly complex, the definition of my task was simple. Learn it.

I stepped into a staff leader's apartment when he came to New York City and found Colonial furniture. In New York you don't do your house in Colonial! There was even a Declaration of Inde-pendence on the wall. I said, "Oh, no." I hate Colonial. A couple of months ago, after I had been ministering in New York City for about four years and was planning to spend my whole life min-istering to the needs there, the Lord spoke to me emphatically and said, "Out to the suburbs." I couldn't believe it. I said, "Are you sure?" He said, "I'm sure." I'll give you one guess what style of architecture is up there—Colonial. God is beating back my ethnocentrism now. I am beginning to learn what bottle collecting, antiquing and collecting old newspapers is all about. I'm learning how to appreciate what these people know and love. And like Elisabeth Elliot I'm keeping my mouth shut.

Where Do We Go from Here?

Where do we go from here? To those who are sympathetic with our desires to share Christ: our parents if possible, our pastor or elders, interested members of our church and our Christian friends. You have to allow others to become part of the blessing of sharing the responsibility of world evangelism. Ask for their prayers and encouragement.

On the way back home, why don't you pick up a new habit, if you don't have it already. Get a newsweekly, a good one like *Time, Newsweek* or *U.S. News & World Report,* one that has an international scope. Begin to acquaint yourself with the world at large and its present crises. If God has been leading you to consider one country especially, cut out the articles about that nation. Keep a notebook with these articles and pray for the national leaders as well as for the believers there.

Where do we go from here? Back to our stationery and ballpoint pens to write letters to individual missionaries. A believer serving Christ and others abroad can give a valuable perspective on a country, a perspective available nowhere else. And your observations and enthusiasm can buoy him up, giving him the joy of knowing that another shares his particular burden.

Where do we go from here? Back to our campuses and churches for experience in group and personal evangelism, discipleship and development of the spirit of willingness. Back to consult with mission boards, finding out specific information about them. Back to plan a summer that is rich in new lessons—lessons derived from watching others share Christ on their soil, their way. Back to those who feel as we do about missions to get their prayer support and their encouragement. Back to get a subscription to a news magazine that will keep us informed of the world at large.

Back to correspond with a missionary to get a unique perspective of the nation to which God is leading us.

Where do we go from here? Back to talk the whole matter over with God some more, cultivating the spirit which says, "Anywhere, Lord, anywhere."

Russell Weatherspoon teaches at the Stony Brook School in New York. He originally gave this address at Urbana 73 which appeared in Jesus Christ: Lord of the Universe, Hope of the World. *© 1974 by Inter-Varsity Christian Fellowship of the U.S.A.*

17

Getting God's Global Perspective

Ruth Siemens

In God's enemy-occupied world, a Christian's inaction is a kind of action. It supports the control of the imposter who dominates this world. For without human accomplices he could do nothing. We may not postpone personal involvement until one day we find ourselves in some distant Timbuktu.

God has already assigned each of us to a current post—to represent him on a campus, in a neighborhood, in a place of employment. This assignment is as important as any we will ever have because it is *God's* place for us *now*. However, this domestic responsibility does not relieve us of our responsibility for international involvement in this global spiritual struggle. Soldiers who do not care about other fronts have not understood what the war is all about and cannot therefore see even their immediate work right.

Where we currently find ourselves in society is important. We must believe that God has hand-picked us and placed us with other hand-picked Christians to work together as a unit, as his representatives in that place. Wars are not won by loners. Together we make known the rightful King in that circle of people among whom he has already placed us.

This present task constitutes a test. Can God ever entrust us with a greater responsibility? This depends on our faithfulness now (Mt. 25:14-30). It doesn't make a lot of sense to pray about God's future will for us if we disregard his current will.

This present task also provides training for our next post. Going overseas will not help you share your faith if you cannot do it here. And international neighbors (student and nonstudent) give us opportunities for cross-cultural communication of the good news right now.

Imagine yourself in Ecuador watching an evangelistic Bible study grow into a discipling Bible study and that turning into a small house church! Now is the time to gain skills in these areas. Experience in small group and large group leadership is valuable missionary training. Take advantage of all the training opportunities God makes available to you like weekend conferences or summer camps.

Do not underestimate the importance of your academic preparation either. Engineering, teaching, nursing, agriculture and many other careers and skills are entry visas to closed areas of the world, whether one goes with a mission board or in a secular position. In open countries it enables you to work side by side with Zambians, Uruguayans or Italians. Through caring relationships you can gain entrance into their lives for Jesus Christ. Can you afford your major? Is it frivolous or selfishly chosen? Or is it useful for God in this needy world he loves? Most solid careers are useful, but every Christian should know why he or she is in a certain field.

Christians today cannot afford the luxury of only one language, even if they never go overseas. God has moved a sizable portion of "the mission field" into our own neighborhoods.

Acquire all the practical skills you can. Can you cook quick, economical, nutritious meals without Betty Crocker's mixes or Ragu spaghetti sauce? Simple electrical repairs, plumbing, carpentry, auto repair—in fact many crafts can prove to be useful later.

Another present responsibility is care of your physical health. You can't be frivolous with your resources and expect to have a big piece left for God after college. This means proper meals, enough sleep and exercise.

What about your current involvement in what God is doing overseas? Prayer enables you to affect people and events half a world away, and it always zeroes in on its target. Letters keep open communication lines to the fronts, and giving keeps the supply lines open. Through summer missionary service and short terms, you can visit the front lines and see for yourself. The effectiveness of all three of these depend on the information you have about the world.

Can you locate these new countries on a map? Sri Lanka, Surinam, Seychelles, Mauritius, Rwanda, Zaire, Papua New Guinea? Over one hundred new countries (more than half of all countries in the world) less than thirty years old send us all back to geography books and atlases. Can you locate these very old countries? Ethiopia, Thailand, Mongolia, Greece? Do you know what's happening today in Nicaragua, Rhodesia, Namibia, Uganda, Afghanistan, Somalia and Mozambique?

How can we pray or give or plan effectively if we don't know that Irian Jaya, part of Indonesia, is now 70% evangelical? Or that France has more Muslims than Christians? Or that Brazil has more Bible-teaching churches than all of France, Belgium, Portugal, Spain, Italy and Austria combined? Or that there is no evangelical church at all in any North African Arab nation? Or that there is no known national Christian in Libya? Unless we have information about countries, we will have no mental pegs on which to hang missionary information, and it will not greatly affect us.

My country-by-country file is now bulging with exciting data from newspapers and news magazines, almanacs, National Geographics and many Christian magazines. We need to know a little about every country and a lot about two or three. I also find it useful in another file to collect material on mission trends and problems.

110

You can take a missions course for credit by correspondence. Inter-Varsity Christian Fellowship's Overseas Training Camp in Central America can give you a good introduction to missions. Or take the preparatory training from Student Training in Missions and have them hand-tailor a situation for you almost anywhere in the world. (Write IVCF, 233 Langdon, Madison, WI 53703 for more information on any of these.) Almost every mission board has a summer program where you give some help as you learn about missions.

There are secular summer opportunities too. How would you like to help a rural Finnish family improve their English in exchange for a summer's room and board? Or help with the fruit harvest in Poland side by side with Polish young people? Or work in a hotel in Switzerland or in a youth camp in France?

Have you thought about studying abroad for a summer, a semester or an academic year? This can be an excellent introduction to another culture and a genuine missionary experience, if you get the right information before you go. What about graduate studies? This is an ideal way to work with students overseas. There are some internships or work-study programs for undergraduates or recent graduates.

There are some one-year work opportunities with mission boards and secular organizations, but not many. It is easier, after graduation, to get a two-year assignment with a mission board, or a two- to three-year contract with a secular organization. (You can get information on all of the above by writing Overseas Counseling Service, 1594 N. Allen, Apt. 23, Pasadena, CA 91104.)

To see our present post in God's world in its right perspective should motivate us to do it with joy. Our current involvement in overseas missions can add a very exciting new dimension to our lives and please our Lord and King.

Ruth Siemens, a staff worker for the International Fellowship of Evangelical Students for many years, is currently a missions specialist for Inter-Varsity Christian Fellowship.

18

Growing an International Friendship

Ned Hale

If your interest in missions has been stirred, one way to put your interest into some very practical learning experiences is to befriend a few international students on your campus. The rewards will be mutual! You will learn a great deal about how to relate to someone from another culture, and you will have the joy of discovering more about God's will for you as a missionary right here and now! The international will benefit immensely by discovering a Christian friend who not only can become like a brother or sister but who also can become the channel by which God's love is seen and felt.

Doing It One to One

First things first. Where can you find international students? Attend the cosmopolitan club or other international student groups to learn about other cultures and to meet students. At the first of the year you can meet them as they arrive on the bus, train or plane. Help them get oriented. Show them around campus. Help them find a residence and map out courses for registration. Explain some of the peculiar customs and traditions you run into.

The next step is to learn to be a true friend. Through trial and error it has been found that the best way to communicate the gospel to international students is by building a personal friendship over a period of time. There are several reasons for this. First, one must presuppose a lack of knowledge in the foreign students about the Scriptures and biblical terms. Second, because of the reputation of some American students' religious backgrounds (legalism, hypocrisy, sensuality and so on), internationals are apt to be distrustful of religious people until they can view the practical application of Christianity to daily life. Finally, their primary emotional need in North American culture is for a close personal relationship with one whom they can implicitly trust.

Therefore a *few* close personal relationships with internationals will accomplish more in the long run. It is safe to say that once a friendship has been fully won with an international student, it is virtually impossible to offend him or her by straightforward witness to the gospel of Christ.

When you start up friendships, be sure to learn full names correctly. Then find out on your own about their country, religion and customs. And don't be interested in them just to preach to them or to use them to speak to groups. If you do not intend to care about them as total persons, it might be best not to initiate the friendship at all.

Once the friendship has begun, there are a variety of ways you can spend time with him or her, helping your relationship to grow. For example, you could study together. Some welcome help with English. (You could also help with English through Bible study in a modern translation.) But realize that while many have learned formal English, they may have trouble understanding colloquial expressions. Or take an international student home with you over the holidays or during vacations. Especially plan to *bring* them to Christian houseparties held at Lake Tahoe, Mt. Baker, Bear Trap Ranch, Cedar Campus or Banff (write IVCF for information).

Lastly, invite your friend to the regular social activities (banquets, picnics and so on) offered by your campus Christian fellowship.

Doing It As a Body

As a group, the place to begin is to commit yourselves to befriend international students. There are some practical ways you can fulfill this commitment.

One is to participate in the brother-sister program on your campus if there is one. If not, your fellowship could push to get one started through the student council or the college administration. This would involve writing to the students during the summer, meeting them when they come by train or bus, helping them to get acquainted with the campus and following through during the year.

Another possibility is to sponsor parties aimed at getting to meet internationals and then following up with personal friendships. Consider having a tea for internationals twice a semester to gain initial contact with internationals on a social level.

If you advertise a speaker on a subject like "Christianity and Its Relevance to the Modern World," only the interested foreign students will attend, narrowing the field for future efforts. The degree of interest in spiritual things can be further narrowed by the speaker's offer of booklets after his talk which students who want further information about Christianity can *sign up for.*

With the names of such students listed with their request for a booklet to be given to them at a later date, you have a perfect opportunity for visiting the student personally, giving him or her the booklet free of charge and finding out in a private conversation where the student is with God. Use this opportunity to build a personal friendship, and invite the students to other situations where Christian friendships can be cultivated and where they can become acquainted with Jesus Christ.

Once a semester, usually at the beginning, a student in your fellowship should visit the dean or whoever is responsible to get permission to use campus facilities for the tea and to advertise it. Invite a speaker and agree on a topic. Then arrange for refreshments to be served and for the advertising to be made and distributed to key places on campus. Then about one week before the tea, send a mimeographed letter to each international student on campus inviting him to the tea. You might be able to get the address of the internationals from the foreign student adviser or the dean. Each Christian should be encouraged to bring at least one international to the tea.

You might also try a foreign dinner in which your campus fellowship buys the food and some internationals from one or two countries work together with your members to teach them how to prepare an international meal.

Or try inviting internationals to the home of a faculty member for a home-cooked meal and to hear the faculty member speak on "What Basic Christianity Is." Most internationals want to learn about Christianity and its relationship to our culture. Encourage informal discussion so that questions may be answered.

Another idea is a progressive dinner in the homes of various Christians from local churches who are interested in befriending foreign students. This can be an excellent way of introducing the Christian community to this ministry. Each Christian student should bring a friend. Internationals usually love to show slides of their country. So an exchange of ideas and customs is a good way to introduce Christianity to them. *Always let them know* before coming if there is to be a short talk on Christianity so they do not feel trapped.

Hospitality after group functions is imperative to maintain vital relationships and confidence. Group activities and individual activities with internationals will make it possible to have internationals over to a home for group Bible studies led by students, faculty or local Christians.

Getting Ready
Preparation for being a genuine friend is a constant process. We *pray* for those we love. We look for practical ways to express our love by *planning* things that are mutually beneficial and interesting to talk about or to do together. *Reading* about a particular student's country, its politics, economics, religion(s), family life and

customs can be a highly rewarding part of the relationship. If you can't find anything to read, you can always ask the international to *tell* you about these things!

There are a few basic resources you can use: (1) The library will produce much information on a country or religion. (2) In an encyclopedia you can look up any country. Just make sure that printing is up to date! (3) *National Geographic Magazine* has colorful articles on most parts of the world. (4) *Operation World* by P. J. Johnstone (Bromley, Kent, England: Send the Light Publications, 1978) gives brief sketches on every continent and country in the world. It also acts as a prayer guide for world evangelization. Order from the William Carey Library, P.O. Box 128-C, Pasadena, CA 91104. (5) *A Guide to International Friendship* by Paul E. Little is a seventeen-page booklet from Inter-Varsity Christian Fellowship. It costs 25¢. Order from IVCF, 233 Langdon St., Madison, WI 53703. (6) Check the InterVarsity Press catalog for books related to the world's religions. You can get one free from IVP, Box F, Downers Grove, IL 60515.

Ned Hale is the central region director for Inter-Varsity Christian Fellowship of the U.S.A.

19

Unless They Are Sent

Melvin J. Friesen

The quarterback racing down the field can do so only with the support of a strong offensive line and the assistance of others down the field. Newscasters can highlight the news only because they rely on a large staff of researchers, script writers and technicians. With excited anticipation we watched men on the moon, not being aware or fully recognizing that thousands of planners, engineers, builders, technicians, computer scientists and people posted at lonely tracking stations around the world made these historic steps possible.

It was realizing this sort of thing that likely caused the apostle Paul after stating that "every one who calls upon the name of the Lord will be saved," to continue, "But how are men to call upon him in whom they have not believed? And how are they to believe in him of whom they have never heard? And how are they to hear without a preacher? And how can men preach unless they are sent? As it is written, 'How beautiful are the feet of those who preach good news!' " (Rom. 10:13-15).

Strange how we single out the one who is sent, the missionary, forgetting those who are responsible for sending him or her. How we revel at the moonwalkers, not appreciating the many who made their journey possible; spotlight the newscaster, unaware of the large back-up crew; are oblivious of the team's scramble, focusing on the quarterback with the ball in hand! We have become a nation, a people, of hero worshipers, keying on the performer, paying small attention to those making it possible for the performer to be limelighted.

But let's get back to Paul's series of questions—simple, obvious, but evidently profound. They follow Paul's reminder that Jesus is Lord and that this "same Lord is Lord of all and bestows his riches upon all who call upon him" (Rom. 10:12).

Jesus began his public ministry reading from the scroll of the prophet Isaiah, "The Spirit of the Lord is upon me, because he has anointed me to preach good news to the poor. He has sent me to proclaim release to the captives and recovery of sight to the blind, to set at liberty those who are oppressed, to proclaim the acceptable year of the Lord" (Lk. 4:18-19). This he did! He then issued the call to follow him. He further declared that "As the Father has sent me, even so I send you" (Jn. 20:21). His concluding mandate was to "go into all the world and preach the gospel" (Mk. 16:15).

In proclaiming this good news we take new heart and courage and comfort knowing that Jesus said, "All authority in heaven and on earth has been given to me. Go therefore and make disciples of all nations, baptizing them in the name of the Father and of the Son and of the Holy Spirit, teaching them to observe all that I have commanded you; and lo, I am with you always, to the close of the age" (Mt. 28:18-20). So we see the Lord Jesus who dramatically went so far out of his way to bring us to God through himself calling his followers in unmistakable terms to pass the word along to each succeeding generation to *also* follow him, to be obedient to all that he has commanded them.

Thus he calls us, we who call ourselves by his name. He calls us to go out of our way to bring others to God through Christ Jesus the Lord, proclaiming and demonstrating his redemptive word to the poor, the enslaved, the sick, the oppressed.

Pondering these directives may well leave us in a quandary. If we are to be involved in all that is implied in "going" and also provide back-up for those who do, why does he seem to call us to a reckless abandon of material goods and possessions? "I tell you, do not be anxious about your life, what you shall eat or what you shall drink, nor about your body, what you shall put on. Is not life more than food, and the body more than clothing?" (Mt. 6:25).

Yet on the other hand, in declaring the cost of being a disciple, Jesus uses two illustrations which show how important it is to give meticulous attention to the ingredients necessary for building a tower or for going to battle. "Which of you, desiring to build a tower, does not first sit down and count the cost, whether he has enough to complete it? . . . Or what king, going to encounter another king in war, will not sit down first and take counsel whether he is able with ten thousand to meet him who comes against him with twenty thousand?" (Lk. 14:28, 31).

Jesus is giving us two important principles to note in following him. On the one hand he is telling us what our attitude about things, material possessions, should be. We are not to be anxious or worry about them. He is our provider: he knows about tomorrow. Don't worry about it. We must sow the seed; only he can germinate it.

When he talks about the cost of discipleship, however, and what is really involved in following him, he uses the very down-to-earth, no-nonsense illustration of the planning needed to bring a task to completion.

In the Old Testament the tithe, or tenth, was a requirement of the faithful, to say nothing of additional gifts and extra offerings scheduled periodically. Compassion for all kinds of disadvantaged is implicit and explicit.

In the New Testament one does not hear so much of the tithe although it was a part of the continuing tradition. Rather a greater

119

emphasis is made on the total ownership of our bodies and possessions by God (for example, Rom. 12:1; 14:7-9; 1 Cor. 6:19-20; Rev. 5:9). Our responsibility, then, is one of returning to him what has come into our custody. That is how Jesus' seemingly contradictory principles come together in one. Whether we go or send, it's all under the awareness of his ownership and our desire to do his bidding. If Jesus is Lord (and he is) and I am his (and I am), then it is not a question of whether I will or will not go or send, but how I should be involved in going or sending or both. I am responsible and accountable to God for all that I am and have.

We must stop putting so much emphasis on the "goer" that we forget all that stands behind him or her. We seem obsessed to magnify the last link. There really are no heroes in God's family the way we tend to identify them. Let's exchange the spotlight for the floodlight and notice all of the unheralded steps and people in obscure corners and behind the scenes. If we did this, we would find other notable ones of whom Christ says, "Well done, good and faithful servant!" (Mt. 25:21).

Wherever we are is a mission field. Yet there are always those beyond our reach who are also our responsibility. Those who remain should learn the seriousness of their stay at home and realize that surely the ninety per cent must send the ten per cent. History bears out the fact that many who go were first those who sent. The whole Christian community needs to fast and pray, to experience the joy of knowing that the Holy Spirit is separating some to go and others to send as in the church in Antioch (Acts 13).

So none of us gets off the hook. All are called. Some are called to go. All are called to pray. All are called to give. When the call to commitment is issued, all should step forward, declaring, "Here am I!" So for all of us, then, you and me, the question really is: How am I going? or how am I sending? No turning back. No turning back.

Melvin J. Friesen is on staff with Inter-Varsity Christian Fellowship in California.

Understanding My Commitment

1. What is my understanding of world mission?

_____

_____

_____

_____

2. What one key thing has God been saying to me about my participation in his world mission?

_____

_____

_____

3. What is my next step in obeying his purpose for me? (Be specific: like getting to know a missionary, writing to him or her, subscribing to a missionary journal, reading a particular book, etc.)

_____

_____

_____

4. In what one thing do I need God's help to activate my next step?

_____

_____

5. Who could I share my commitment with and my need for prayer? His or her name is _____
What day will I do this? _____
Write to the I-V Missions Department for further help:
Inter-Varsity Missions, 233 Langdon, Madison, WI 53703

Questions for Discussion

If we are honest with ourselves about the implications of discipleship, of following Jesus Christ, we must grapple with what Christ says about the world mission of the church. One way to do this is through a group discussion of the present book.

The following questions are designed to help a group move through some of the relevant issues. There are ten studies, six on the articles in the book and four Bible studies. Each fits comfortably in a 45- to 60-minute time slot. The members of the group should read each article or passage before coming to the discussion.

An outline for using this book with a group might look as follows:

The questions provide a skeleton on which to hang discussion. This allows the leader freedom to adapt each study to the flow of discussion through follow-up questions and the like. Scattered throughout are application questions which personalize the discussion and keep it from constantly being theoretical.

Although summary questions are provided only at the end in the form of "Understanding My Commitment," after each discussion the leader is encouraged to summarize the main points the group has brought out.

A leader need not have "all the answers" but rather should lead the people in the group to discover for themselves what is involved in the Great Commission. (Helpful general suggestions for leading group discussions are found in James Nyquist's *Leading Bible Discussions*, especially chapter eight. This is available from InterVarsity Press.)

Discussion 1

Missions and Evangelism: Is There a Difference?

1. The words *missions* and *evangelism* are often used interchangeably. However, Tuggy sees them differently. How does he define *evangelism?* When does evangelism happen? How do you know it has happened?

2. Why does Tuggy insist that the second word, *missions,* must be distinguished from *evangelism?*

3. Define *missions* in your own words to show that it is related to but distinct from *evangelism.*

4. Are all Christians "missionaries"? What makes you a missionary?

The Living God Is a Missionary God

1. Why, according to Stott, is it important to know on what grounds the Christian mission rests?

What other reasons can you think of?

2. What was the context of God's promise to Abraham?

How was the promise of a land, a posterity and a blessing fulfilled in the past?

How is the promise receiving fulfillment in the present?

How will God's promise to Abraham receive its final fulfillment in the future?

3. Looking at Stott's conclusion, what do we learn about God from his promise to Abraham and its fulfillment?

How can knowing these things be motivating as you consider your role in God's plan for the world?

Take time to praise God for the things you've learned about him.

Discussion 2

What in the World Is God Doing?

1. Kane is full of enthusiasm for the world mission of the church. Where does he see it headed?

2. What are some of the reasons for the rapid growth of the church in the past twenty-five years? What problem prevents the completion of world evangelization?

3. Do you share Kane's enthusiasm? Why or why not?

The Need in World Mission Today

1. How does Winter define *normal* evangelism?

What is crosscultural evangelism?

2. Explain what is represented by each of the four circles in

Figure 1 on page 41.

How do you feel about the size of the task remaining?

3. Among the three major blocs, which has the greatest need for evangelism?

How does the rest of the world differ from the three major blocs?

4. Why do you think most of the energies of the church are focused on those who already consider themselves Christians?

Have you ever attempted to witness to someone outside your cultural sphere?

If so, what was it like?

5. What are some ways the church could attempt to reach more effectively those who do not call themselves Christians?

Discussion 3
The Messenger's Qualifications

1. What is Magalit's response to those who say the day of the Western missionary is coming to an end? What attitudes does he suggest an American missionary must have today?

2. Briefly describe the three qualifications Magalit says are essential.

What is the scriptural basis of each?

Why is each of these qualities so crucial in missionary work?

3. What can you do to develop each of the qualities mentioned by Magalit?

4. What does partnership in missions mean? How do some American missionaries thwart partnership? How can this be avoided?

That Amazing Thing Called the Church

1. MacDonald acknowledges that the church does not always seem relevant to the average student. Has this been your experience? Explain.

2. MacDonald goes on to list six principles that show the church to be central to God's working in our world. Briefly summarize each of the six principles.

What is the basis for these principles?

3. What can you say about the role of the local church in light of this article?

125

Does your church fill this role? Explain.

4. What determines the effectiveness of the local church? (See the fifth principle.)

How can you help your church to be more effective in fulfilling its mission? Be specific.

5. Why is it important that you be involved in the church?

Discussions 4-7 See part two (pp. 71-81).

Discussion 8
Undebatable Guidance

1. What are some ways God can guide us?

Which is the clearest and most certain?

2. When do you have difficulty following his certain will?

How can consistently following God's obvious will help us to know how to act when his guidance is not so clear?

3. Briefly, what are the three principles in Romans 12:1-2 for knowing God's will?

How can each of these principles help you discern God's will?

4. Do you disagree with any of the five principles found at the end of Oerter's article? Explain.

5. What factors do you need to keep in mind as you try to find out whether God wants you involved in crosscultural evangelism?

Before You Go; Once You're There; Hints for Handling an Abnormal Blessing; Talking with Mission Agencies

1. Why would it be a good idea to prepare for Urbana?

What are some of the suggestions Evans-Layng gives for preparing for Urbana?

2. What are some of the draining experiences Treguboff says you could face at Urbana?

3. Which of Hammond's hints would you say is most important? Why?

4. In Shingledecker's and Rutz's article, what factors seem most crucial for you as you investigate various mission agencies?

5. How can attending Urbana be a parable of a missionary experience?

If you are going to Urbana, what steps will you take to get ready before you go?

Discussion 9
Cultivating That Anywhere Spirit
1. What does Weatherspoon say are the two prerequisites for missions?
If you are weak in either area, what suggestions does he give for strengthening it?
2. What is ethnocentrism?
What causes it?
How can it be rectified?
3. How might you be ethnocentric?
Be honest. If you don't know if you are ethnocentric or not, how can you find out?

Getting God's Global Perspective
1. What analogy does Siemens use to describe Christians in the world?
Do you think it is a good analogy?
Why or why not?
2. Why should you consider your schooling and your hobbies in light of God's global perspective?
How would you evaluate these now?
3. Why is it important to get information on the different countries of the world?
What are some ways Siemens suggests you can do this?

Growing an International Friendship
1. Have you ever known an international well?
How did you get to know him or her?
How did your friendship grow?
What did you learn about yourself in the process?
If you have never had an international friend, what fears do you have as you think about making one?
2. Why do you think internationals respond to the gospel best in the context of friendships with Christians?

3. Which of the suggestions that Hale gives do you think would work best for your fellowship group? Explain.

Discussion 10
Unless They Are Sent
1. Why do people tend to focus on the person in the spotlight rather than on all those who made the achievement possible? How have we tended to do this as Christians?
How does the lordship of Christ challenge such thinking?
2. Friesen mentions two illustrations that Christ gives about handling possessions. What are they?
Why do they seem to have opposite conclusions?
How are they, in fact, reconciled into one?
3. What then are the responsibilities of every Christian as regards God's world mission?
In which of these responsibilities have you been weak?

Understanding My Commitment
1. Throughout this series on mission you have had an opportunity to pray and think about your own role in God's purposes for the world. Here is a way you can solidify before God what you have learned. Take a couple of minutes to write an answer to question 1. Who is involved? For whom are they responsible? For what are they responsible? To whom are they responsible?
2. Now take a couple of minutes for question 2. Write down one key thing God has been speaking about to you. Don't list many. Choose one.
3. Now look at question 3. Be specific. (And so on with 4-5. See the World Evangelism Decision Card in the appendix for a possible next step.)
4. Would anyone like to share what they've written? Let's pray for each other's commitments. (Or break up into pairs. Have each take two or three minutes to share what they've written, and then another five or ten minutes to pray for each other.)

Appendix A: *World Evangelism Decision Card*

Through the years God has used the IVCF World Evangelism Decision Card (in various forms, colors and wordings) to confront students with the need to make a personal decision in response to Christ's commission to "go . . . and make disciples of all nations."

During the Urbana convention, you, too, will be given a World Evangelism Decision Card and be asked to consider before God what personal commitment he would have you make to his world mission. This decision card is reproduced here so that you may be familiar with it and be prepared to respond to it when it is presented at Urbana. Copies of the decision card may be obtained by writing: Inter-Varsity Missions, 233 Langdon, Madison, WI 53703.

World Evangelism Decision Card

I acknowledge that:

1. All men without Christ are lost but God in love has given His son that they may have eternal life.

2. Jesus Christ is my Lord and Savior and I earnestly desire to recognize His Lordship in every area of my life

3. His command is to go and make disciples of all nations, and I accept that command as my personal responsibility, whether God leads me to go abroad or stay at home

(Check your decision)

☐ **I.** I believe it is God's will for me to serve Him abroad, and I will pray and make inquiry to this end

☐ **II.** Convinced that I have a part in God's plan for the world, I will actively seek His will for me by increasing my awareness of an involvement in world missions.

As a viable indication of my commitment, I will: (select no more than three options)

☐ **A.** Pray daily for specific mission concerns
☐ **B.** Read one or more books about world missions
☐ **C.** Begin a systematic study about world missions
☐ **D.** Join a missions study/action group
☐ **E.** Subscribe to a missions periodical/bulletin
☐ **F.** Develop a friendship with an International student
☐ **G.** Begin to financially and prayerfully support a missionary/national worker
☐ **H.** Make plans to participate in a summer mission program
☐ **I.** Begin corresponding with one or more mission agencies about service opportunities
☐ **J.** Seek further training for preparation to become a missionary

---

My Signature   Date

In signing this card, you indicate a desire to discover, and willingness to obey, God's purpose for your life in terms of Christ's commission to "go . . . and make disciples of all nations."

We are pleased to help you in fulfilling your resolve and will send you material designed to assist you. As you correspond with us, we are ready to counsel you personally about openings, mission boards, further preparation and any other specific matters related to your life-work.

Inter-Varsity Christian Fellowship
Student Missions Fellowship
Nurses Christian Fellowship

233 Langdon Street, Madison, WI 53703

745 Mt. Pleasant Road
Toronto, Ontario M4S 2N5

Printed In USA

Appendix B: Mission Services of Inter-Varsity

Inter-Varsity Christian Fellowship is committed to helping students and recent graduates to promote the world mission of the church and to assisting them as they determine their own role in that mission. To achieve this purpose, Inter-Varsity offers the following services to you.

Summer Training Programs

Overseas Training Camp—a one month crosscultural learning and service experience in the Third-World environment of Central America.

Missions Discipleship Camp—a one month program combining studies on the world of missions with training in basic discipleship and leadership skills, put in a world dimension. Concludes with an urban crosscultural experience.

Student Training in Missions—includes four weekends of crosscultural communications training from January thru April, an eight- to twelve-week summer experience overseas, and a weekend of debriefing in the fall. Applications must be in by November 27.

IVCF also offers a service to help you find specific summer mission programs that fit your own needs and concerns. Write for a form called "So You're Interested in Summer Missions."

Missions Conferences

Urbana Student Missions Convention—this five-day, end-of-December conference is held every two years on the campus of the University of Illinois. The conference brings together thousands of students to participate in a variety of plenary addresses, elective seminars and small group discussions centering on the world mission of the church.

Urbana Onward—a weekend event designed to help recent Urbana participants make application of the things they learned about world missions, in their personal lives and in the life of their chapter or church. Urbana Onward weekends are offered throughout the United States in the few months following each Urbana convention.

Breakthrough: Explorations into World Christian Discipleship—a weekend event that is primarily motivational; helping people to catch a strong sense of how God can use all of us in Christ's global cause. Practical applications and first steps are also explored.

Converge: Becoming Chapters and Churches of World Christians—a sequel to Breakthrough. During this weekend, groups come together to discover how a world dimension can be integrated into everything they are and do. Plans are layed for making a corporate impact on the ends of the earth.

Life with a Purpose—A team of career missionaries are brought together to lead in a weekend of exploration and discussion on crosscultural ministries. Primarily for those serious about investigating such a possibility for their own lives.

Missions Resources

Recommended Reading on the World Mission of the Church—an annotated bibliography on world missions covering: biblical basis, personal preparation, biography, current issues, history, strategy and other topics.

Magazines for World Christians—a listing of some of the best periodicals available, both secular and from mission agencies, to help build your world vision.

Directory of Foreign Mission Agencies—an alphabetical listing of major mission agencies indicating countries in which they work and including addresses and phone numbers of home offices.

In the Gap: What It Means to Be a World Christian—describes what World Christians are, how they think, what they choose and how they take action for Christ's global cause. Includes a wealth of ideas and resources for developing a World Christian lifestyle. Provides the framework for the World Christian booklets. (270 pages, $5.95)

World Christian Booklets—a series of books to help build a world vision, obey the vision and share the vision. Titles include: "World Christian Check-Up," "World Christian Chapter/Church Profile," "Obey the Vision through Prayer," "Magazines for World Christians," "How to Create World Christian Bible Studies," "How to Interview a Real Live Missionary" and "Set World Christian Dreams Free."

World Missions Sourcebook—a compilation of selected articles that give an overview of ideas and debates presently going ～ ～ ～ ～ ～ ～ ～ ～ ～ 'ith discussion questions for each). Also inc' ～ ～ ～ ～ ～ ～ ～ lan booklets. (375 pages, $20.00)

World Evangelism Decision Card—u～ ～ ～ ～ ～ ～ ～ ～ ～ ～ .1eir thinking about and commitment to world miss～ ～ ～ ～ ～ used at Urbana. When the second half of the c ar ～ is r～ ～ ～ ～ ～ ～ ～ ～ .1y, appropriate follow-up material is sent free o~ charge.

Ten Next Steps—a fo～～w-up too～ ～ the World Evangelism Decision Card which details specific res～ ～ ～ ～ ～ s and ide～ ～ help individuals take action in any of the ten options mentioned on the card.

Helps for Your Missions Group

Balanced Missions Emphasis—a paper which describes objectives of a missions emphasis and gives many suggestions for chapter involvement and programs.

IVCF Missions Handbook—a compilation of papers to provide any IVCF chapter with a wealth of information, resources, program ideas and training approaches. ($6.00)

Student Missions Leaders Handbook—a training manual for developing and encouraging missions groups on Christian college campuses—SMF. ($6.00)

Recommended Missionaries/Mission Leaders for a Campus Ministry—a listing of currently available missionaries. Updated annually.

Missions Media

TWENTYONEHUNDRED productions (the multimedia ministry of IVCF) has produced a number of media presentations which provide practical insights into the church's world mission and stimulus for participation in world missions. These presentations are designed for churches, conferences and schools as well as student group meetings, and are available on a rental basis. The media presentations operate only on the Pocket Star 2-projector system: available on an advance-reservation basis from local IVCF staff. For rental details and a brochure describing the media presentations now available, write: TWENTY-ONEHUNDRED, 233 Langdon, Madison, WI 53703.

Overseas Counseling Service (OCS)

An information and counseling service for those seriously considering overseas ministry as a nonprofessional missionary (self-supporting witness). OCS has computerized information on thousands of positions all over the world. Write: Overseas Counseling Service, 1594 N. Allen #23, Pasadena, CA 91104.

For further information about any of these missions services, write: Inter-Varsity Missions, 233 Langdon, Madison, WI 53703.